# HISTORIC Churches SYNAGOGUES & SPIRITUAL PLACES *of* EASTERN MAINE

# HISTORIC Churches SYNAGOGUES & SPIRITUAL PLACES *of* EASTERN MAINE

JIM & JANE DIGGINS HARNEDY

THE History PRESS

Published by The History Press
Charleston, SC 29403
www.historypress.net



*Back cover: Spiritual Path*, 11x17 inches acrylic painting by Jane Diggins Harnedy.

Cover design by Karleigh Hambrick.

First published 2011

Manufactured in the United States

ISBN 978.1.59629.409.7

Library of Congress Cataloging-in-Publication Data

Harnedy, Jim.
Historic churches, synagogues, and spiritual places of eastern 203/.5093-203/.5099 / Jim and Jane Diggins Harnedy.
p. cm.
ISBN 978-1-59629-409-7
1. Maine--Church history. 2. Church buildings--Maine. I. Harnedy, Jane Diggins. II. Title.
BR555.M2H37 2011
203'.5097414--dc23
2011017905

# Contents

## 3. A Faith of Our Fathers Tour Way Down East



## 4. Passamaquoddy and Penobscot Spiritual Traditions

# Preface

The place we call Maine today has a rich spiritual tapestry. For eons, Native Americans practiced a spiritual sensibility that kept their lives totally attuned with their environment. In 1604, Pierre Dugua, Samuel Champlain and seventy-seven other men established the first European settlement north of St. Augustine, Florida, and brought Christianity to this New World settlement, Way Down East, on St. Croix Island near Calais, Maine. This settlement can truly be called an ecumenical one, as a Catholic priest and a Huguenot Protestant minister provided for the spiritual needs of the men. You will discover that if it were not for the help that the local Passamaquoddys provided, the entire ill-fated colony would have perished during the winter of 1605.

Through the years, the major religious traditions of the world have found a home here and offered us a living proof of a power beyond our comprehension. Our book will guide you to a number of interesting houses of worship and unique religious sites of many denominations throughout Greater Bangor, Acadia and Way Down East.

You will learn of the disastrous fire of April 30, 1911, that swept through Bangor and destroyed many of the Queen City's houses of worship, including Congregation Beth Israel's first shul, Maine's oldest Jewish house of worship. In the small coastal town of Surry, you will find an authentic Japanese-style zendo for people of any background or faith to practice Buddhist meditation. Bar Harbor's Maine Sea Coast Mission will introduce you to the special ministry founded in 1905 by two brothers who were both Congregational ministers that were dedicated to making a difference in the difficult lives of those souls living on Down East Maine's outer islands. History abounds in the houses of worship found Way Down East. Here you will find both the important spiritual and civic roles the Centre Street Congregational Church of Machias have played since Revolutionary days, the special place that St. Joseph's Catholic Church in Eastport has occupied and how two American presidents and a Canadian prime minister have all worshipped at St. Anne's small Anglican church on Campobello Island. These are but a few selections of what you will discover on your journey through our book.

The Hindu spiritual tradition says that to be a Hindu means to be traveling somewhere along the path to sainthood. Spirituality has as its core the concept of travel. Each of us must find that special road or path that whispers to one's soul that you're headed in the right direction. A road that takes you to a historic church or synagogue may rekindle the religious faith that you were raised in but somehow left along the way. A religious site that you discover in a peaceful, secluded and spiritually nurturing setting may well be the catalyst for raising your spirit to its connection with the Supreme Being.

We encourage you to spend some time away from your busy commitments to explore some of the houses of worship here in eastern Maine that especially appeal to your religious and/or spiritual interests.

# Acknowledgements


## Spiritual Paths through Greater Bangor

Evelyn Clisham, Tina Farril, Steven Gatchell. Dr. Reverend James L. Haddix, Joan Hei, Reverend Elaine Hewes, Carolyn Hopkins, Brother Kenneth Leo, Rabbi David Lerner, Nancy Long, Reverend Cathy Macedo, Mary Ann McGuire, Reverend Adam Metropolis, Reverend Brad Mitchell, Reverend Timothy J. Nadeau, Brother Donald Paul, Ruth Perry, W. Reid, Carmen Rice, Reverend Stephanie Salinas, Teresa K. Sprague, Stacey Sterling, Reverend Roger Tracy and Carolyn Kinnard Ziffer.

## Acadia's Religious Heritage

Reverend David Andrews, Reverend Jonathan Appleyard, Sara Clemens, Hugh Curran, Reverend Nicholas Davis III, Reverend Gary A. DeLong, Reneé Graves, Mary Agnes McGuire, Rachael Monk, Reverend Scott Mower, Reverend John O'Hara, Stephen H. Richards, Reverend Leela Rajani Sinha, Wayne Smith and Reverend Mark Worth.

## A FAITH OF OUR FATHERS TOUR WAY DOWN EAST

John and Marge Ahlin, Dot Gaddis, Reverend Gene Gaffey, Timothy Harrison, Francis Libby, Reverend Francois Akoa-Mongo, Reverend Frank Morin, Reverend Mark Nolette, Reverend Ed Randall, Donna Rau, Alahna Roach, John Sawyer, Reverend Patti Sears, Reverend Charles Smart, Reverend David Sivret and Pastor Donald Wood.

## PASSAMAQUODDY AND PENOBSCOT SPIRITUAL TRADITIONS

Pat Phillips Doyle, Juliana L'Heureux, Reverend Paul Kerns, Reverend Frank Morin and Sister Janice Murphy.

A special thanks to our daughter, Susan J. Blackwell, for her editorial and technical assistance.

*Chapter 1*

# Spiritual Paths through Greater Bangor

## Bangor

### *All Souls Congregational Church*

All Souls Church was formed in 1912 as the result of the Great Bangor Fire of 1911, which destroyed both the First Church of Bangor and the Central Congregational Church. The two congregations voted to unite and form a church they would call All Souls.

The Congregational tradition has rich religious roots both in Bangor and New England. The First Church, Bangor, was gathered in 1811 and was the first parish in the city. The church's traditions can be traced back to early colonial times to the pilgrims and Puritans.

All Souls is a local church of the United Church of Christ, a union of Congregational-Christian churches and the Synod of the Evangelical and Reformed Church. The object of All Souls is to bind together Christian people for the purpose of sharing in the worship of God and making the will of God dominant in the lives of all persons, individually and collectively, especially as that will is set forth in the life, teachings, death and resurrection of Jesus Christ.

Members of All Souls Congregational Church come from many communities in the Greater Bangor area. They share a common faith and strong commitment to family life and to service to the community. Worship is central to their Christian community. It is directed to God, who created all things, and through Jesus Christ, who seeks to redeem his creatures. Worship reminds them of Jesus's commands and empowers people to live according to his leading. Worship services are open to all and may be a source of stimulation, challenge, comfort and strength to those who come and join. Ushers, or greeters, are at the door each Sunday and are most happy to answer any questions that you might have. Downstairs in the vestry, a table is prepared for visitors, where one can also find someone to answer questions.

While all acknowledge that the church is its people, most also agree that a church's art gives pleasure, joy and inspiration to its worshippers. All Souls Meetinghouse is no exception. It has twenty-six beautiful stained glass windows that are truly a work of art that provides another dimension for an individual to appreciate while worshipping.

All Souls Congregational Church provides both money and services to the poor and marginalized segments of society. Among the recipients of their charitable acts are the Seaman's Friend Society, the Ecumenical

All Souls Congregational Church was formed in 1912 as a result of the Great Bangor Fire of 1911. The church is located at 10 Broadway in downtown Bangor.

Food Pantry, Good Shepherd Food Bank, Shaw House, Greater Bangor Area Shelter, Dorothy Day Soup Kitchen, Family of Friends and Makers of Meals and Habitat for Humanity.

Worship services are held each Sunday. Nursery care is provided. Church school meets concurrent with morning worship. All are invited for coffee and fellowship immediately after Sunday worship.

Throughout the year, church members meet each Thursday at 12:30 p.m. in the chapel to offer prayers of intercession. All are welcome.

All Souls Congregational Church is located at 10 Broadway in downtown Bangor. The Reverend James L. Haddix, Ph.D., minister, and the Reverend Renee U. Garrett, M.Div., minister of Christian nurture, are pleased to make an appointment to talk to people about the church, its beliefs and programs. One can connect by telephone at (207) 942-7354, fax at (207) 942-6535 or their website at www.allsoulsbangor.org.

### *Grace United Methodist Church*

The roots of Methodism in Bangor dates to 1814, based upon *A History of Methodism in Maine*, written in 1886 by Stephen Allen and W.H. Pillsbury, two Methodist ministers in Maine. They document in their book that a Reverend Benjamin Jones formed the first class of eleven laymen in Bangor in 1814.

The Reverend Benjamin Jones was born in Sandwich, Massachusetts, in 1786. At age eleven, he heard Jesse Lee preach, which influenced him to convert a few years later. In 1808, he was licensed to preach, and in 1809, he was admitted to the New England Conference and appointed to the Union Circuit in the District of Maine.

Working as a preacher on the Hampden Circuit, the Reverend Jones preached every four weeks in Bangor at an old schoolhouse at the corner of State and Pine Streets. During the early nineteenth century, people of the Greater Bangor area were most concerned with changing a wilderness into settled farms and small communities. There was little interest in religion. The few interested souls there were belonged to the established church. Methodist ministers were regarded by the regular clergy as intruders at best and preachers of heresy that should have every possible obstacle thrown in their path. It is within that historical context that Methodism made its humble start in Bangor.

When the Reverend Jones came to Bangor in 1814 to organize a Methodist class, he was just twenty-eight years old. For the next forty-two years, his ministry witnessed a great number of conversions as a direct result of his tireless labors. In 1850, at age sixty-four, the Reverend Jones died in Lincolnville, Maine.

During these early years of the 1800s, Methodist pastoral oversight was limited by the large size of the circuit. Thus, no significant numerical gains in Methodist converts were recorded by the Methodist Society of Bangor. In 1827, a turning point in the affairs of the society took place. In that year, members of the society were stirred to begin building a meetinghouse, and some forty people were converted to Methodism.

This first church was completed in 1828 at a cost of $4,500. In November 1828, the Reverend Charles Baker, the presiding elder, dedicated the new meetinghouse. It appears that it was a fairly large building for the number of parishioners at the time. Although church records state that this first church was built on Summer Street, contradictory statements claim that the church was actually at the intersection of Union and Independent Streets. In 1856, the church building was abandoned and sold as commercial property for $5,000.

In 1835, Maine Methodists meeting in Bangor placed themselves squarely on the side of states' rights, which put them in support of the south's position of advocating and defending a cautious approach to the whole question of slavery. This position placed them in direct opposition to William Lloyd Garrison and his followers in that branch of the Methodist church, which was boldly speaking out against slavery. A serious division occurred during the period leading up to the Civil War, focusing on the issue of how far the church could go in accepting the status quo and when it was time to speak out with a prophetic voice.

Maine Methodists moved a great step from its resolution of 1835 with its disclaimer of any individual or church responsibility for slavery and its defense of states' rights against the federal government. This is all part of Bangor Methodism.

Despite the serious division within the church at the time, 1854 proved to be a good year for the Old Meeting House Society. About 120 were converted or reclaimed, and a new church building was begun on Union Street (the present Grace United Methodist Church Building). After being completed in 1855, it was dedicated on November 15 of that year. When the cornerstone was laid, it marked the celebration of forty years of Methodism in Bangor.

Grace United Methodist Church had a primarily wood exterior until a stone facing was added in 1948; it celebrated its $150^{th}$ anniversary in 2004. The church brings its Christian message to the greater local community by providing a thrift shop, meals for a homeless shelter and food for an ecumenical cupboard.

Grace United Methodist Church is located at 193 Union Street, Bangor, Maine. The Reverend Kathy Macedo is pastor and can be reached for church services information by telephone at (207) 942-8320 or via e-mail at graceumc193@yahoo.com.

Grace United Methodist Church was dedicated on November 15, 1855.

### *Unitarian Universalist Society of Bangor*

There are three distinct chapters in the church's history. From 1818 until 1995, the Independent Congregational Society–Unitarian's was a prominent Bangor house of worship on the corner of Union and Main Streets. Prior to the nineteenth century, Unitarianism was considered to be a liberal school of thought within New England Congregationalism. Before and after becoming a separate denomination in the 1800s, it attracted a strong following within the intellectual and cultural leadership of New England. Among the early Unitarian ministers here in Bangor was Dr. Frederick Henry Hedge, a scholar and transcendentalist friend of Ralph Waldo Emerson. Prior to the Civil War era, the Reverend Joseph Henry Adams was an active abolitionist and preacher against slavery. Hannibal Hamlin, a graduate of the Bangor Theological Seminary, Abraham Lincoln's first vice president (from 1861 to 1865), as well as a Maine governor and U.S. senator, was an active member of the Unitarian congregation. During the 1930s, the Reverend Stephen H. Fritchman assailed anti-Semitism and militarism. The congregation was represented in the Civil Rights March in Selma, Alabama, by John Wood. Human dignity was always a solid commitment of the Bangor Unitarian community. When a young, openly gay friend of the congregation was killed, they advocated forcefully against violence and for the dignity of all. In 1995, the Unitarians voted to consolidate with the First Universalist Church.

Like the Unitarians, the Universalist Church in America's roots can also be found in New England. The establishment of the first church was in 1780 in Gloucester, Massachusetts. An organization of churches was formed in 1785, and a convention five years later drew up a statement of faith and adopted the congregational form of government.

In 1833, the First Universalist Society was established in Bangor. From 1833 through the early 1840s, the fledgling congregation met in various locations but did not record much in the way of their activities. Church history does document that two ministers served the congregation from 1840 to 1850. For one year, 1840 to 1841, the Reverend L.L. Sadler led the flock, and from 1843 to 1850, the Reverend A.R. Nye ministered to the congregation. A small building was erected by the society as a house of worship in 1844.

In 1850, the Reverend Amory Battles came to the church. For the next twenty-one years, the Reverend Battles was to make a significant imprint on the lives of people and to make his influence felt forever on the institution that he had come to serve. He was an eloquent preacher, an educator and a gentle pastor, as well as a staunch abolitionist who refused by duty of conscience to take an oath to support the Constitution and laws of the United States, as by so doing it would infer that he would uphold the Fugitive Slave Act. During the period of his ministry, the building that was to be the predecessor to the present church was erected. The cornerstone was laid on June 25, 1860, and was dedicated on December 15, 1862. Because of ill health, the Reverend Battles resigned his pastorate in 1871. Succeeding years were devoted to worship, fellowship, community service, Bible study and children's welfare. During this period, the devotion of one layman stands out as preeminent: General Samuel F. Hersey. General Hersey was a prominent Bangor businessman whose philanthropic gifts to the Queen City's Public Library and City Hall were well known. His devotion and generosity to the First Universalist Church were even greater. He had a great love of children, and his bequest to the church of a trust to purchase a tract of land on Penobscot Bay to erect a seaside resort made it possible to provide free summer vacations through the years to thousands of Sunday school youngsters ages six to eighteen.

Shortly after the installation of the Reverend Ashley A. Smith as pastor, the Great Bangor Fire of April 30, 1911, completely destroyed the church building. It was the first of seven Bangor houses of worship to be lost. The Reverend Smith did valiant work in saving a number of cherished articles, including the Bible, Communion silver and pictures until he was driven out by flames. His home was also lost in the fire. During the remainder of the year, weekly services were held at two local theaters. In January 1912, the Unitarians offered the Universalists the use of their church for services at two thirty each Sunday afternoon. Beginning in May 1912, services were held in the newly completed Park Street Church vestry, while the rest of the new church building was being finished. In September, the main auditorium of the new church was used for the first time. The new church's outstanding stained glass windows memorialized the strengths of the previous century and depicted the beliefs of the Universalists. In 1924, the Reverend Smith dedicated the Dorothy Memorial Hall in memory of his daughter. Starting in 1934, a close co-operation grew between the Universalists and Unitarians through the Free Church Fellowship.

During the 1960s, modern memorial windows were installed in the vestry. In the 1980s, the Reverend Gary Smith encouraged the congregation to join the Unitarian Universalist Association and to affirm diversity. This was realized during the 1990s through the ministry of the Reverend Patricia Carol.

The two churches consolidated as the Unitarian Universalist Society in 1995 and initiated their first joint worship on Sunday, September 17, 1995, in the Park Street Church. Most of the cherished religious possessions of the Unitarians were integrated with those of the Universalists, and the Unitarian building was sold. The congregation continues at the dawn of the twenty-first century to support its strong tradition of social action, education and worship, including its commitment to the free Saturday meal program for the hungry of the community.

The Unitarian Universalist Society is located at 120 Park Street, Bangor, Maine. For additional information, contact the church by telephone at (207) 947-7009 or via e-mail at uubangor@aol.com.

Unitarian Universalist Society of Bangor was dedicated in 1913.

## *Columbia Street Baptist Church*

In May 1845, a small group of young parishioners of the First Baptist Church of Bangor opened a mission in Grey's Hall, which was known as "Old Bethel" on Broad Street. Their mission was to minister to the destitute and tough lumberjacks who worked and lived in Bangor's waterfront area, as at that time Bangor was the largest lumber shipping port in the world.

A description of Old Bethel reads: "The eight years during which this church worshiped in the bare old hall, with its straight backed, unpainted wooden benches, its uncarpeted floors and whale-oil lamps, were most fruitful in good results."

On September 12, 1845, the recently opened mission was organized as a church with twenty-seven members. The Reverend Charles G. Porter of Frankfort, Maine, became the pastor of the new church. During the following year, Mrs. Porter wrote to her mother about her joy of seeing their new church congregation grow from two to three hundred souls and that they now needed to find a larger house of worship.

A new and spacious sanctuary that was known as the "Free House" on Columbia Street was officially dedicated on June 15, 1854. The large letters on the front of the building, with the words "Free House" inscribed on it, communicated the fact that all seats were free and that no rental charges would be made.

Through the years, this historic downtown Bangor church has seen many major renovations and improvements through the faithful stewardship of the church family. In 1902, the steep steps of the original building were removed, and the front of the church was totally redesigned. Two towers and stained glass windows were also added during this major building project. The Estey pipe organ and a new baptistery gracing the front of the sanctuary were added in 1928. Other significant improvements including organ chimes, a bell carillon, a sound system and hearing-assisted devices have been added to enhance worship.

To enlarge space, two wings were added during the years 1955–56, and in 1962, the abutting Nissen Building was purchased and renovated to provide the church with classroom space, nursery, staff offices and gymnasium. The gift of an elevator has significantly improved access in the facility for those who have difficulty with stairs.

The Columbia Street Baptist Church was officially dedicated on June 15, 1854, and was known as the "Free House."

For over a century and a half, the Columbia Street Baptist Church has been serving the spiritual needs of the Greater Bangor community at 63 Columbus Street. For additional information, contact the church by telephone at (207) 945-6616 or via e-mail at email@csbcbangor.org.

## *St. John's Catholic Church*

The history of the church is closely intertwined with that of the Queen City. The first record of a Roman Catholic presence in Bangor dates to 1798 when Father Jean Louis Lefebvre Cheverus, a Jesuit missionary, celebrated the first recorded Mass in the city. Assigned to Pleasant Point, Father Cheverus offered the Mass as a thank-you for the hospitality that one of Bangor's first citizens, Seth Buswell, had provided.

During the 1830s, Irish immigrants began arriving in the Queen City to work in the burgeoning lumber industry. To care for the spiritual needs of these new arrivals, Father Patrick McNamee was assigned in 1832 as the first resident priest. Two years later, St. Michael's became the first Catholic church in Bangor. It was built between Court and Ohio Streets.

The decade between 1840 and 1850 saw a surge in Bangor's population as a result of the city becoming the nation's largest lumber exporter. A large percentage of the population growth was due to Irish immigrants seeking job opportunities here. A backlash to the rapid growth of the Irish immigrant population occurred. This anti-Irish sentiment was encouraged by a semisecret fraternal organization turned political party known as the Know-Nothings, which opposed certain immigrant groups, including Catholics. Their name came from the fact that members professed ignorance of the party's activities. On Saturday, October 14, 1854, Father John Bapst, a Swiss Jesuit whose ministry tended to the spiritual needs of Indians, Canadian and Irish settlers in Eastern Maine, was seized by a mob, stripped of his clothes and tarred and feathered. Ironically, it was this violence by the Know-Nothings that led to the establishment of St. John the Evangelist Catholic Church in Bangor.

On December 8, 1854, the cornerstone of St. John's Catholic Church was laid on York Street in what at that time was in the center of the city's "Irish ghetto." Beneath the cornerstone, a bottle was placed that contained a piece of Father Bapst's tarred, feathered and bloodstained cassock. A fully recovered Father Bapst presided over the first Mass on Christmas Day 1855 in the basement of the unfinished church. Father Bapst went on to become a founder and first president of Boston College.

During the remaining nineteenth century, the parish flourished both spiritually and physically. Specifically, a rectory, convent and school were built. Later, the steeple was added, with its 3,400-pound bell. The beautiful Tyrolean stained glass windows that graphically portray biblical stories were designed by Franz Xavier Pernlochner and installed in the church between 1885 and 1888.

In 1973, St. John's Catholic Church was placed on the National Register of Historic Places. As part of the Year 2000 Jubilee, St. John's, together with five other Catholic churches in Maine, was selected for a special role in ushering in the new millennium.

St. John's celebrated in 2005 its 150$^{th}$ anniversary serving the spiritual needs of Bangor Catholics. The Most Reverend Richard J. Malone, bishop of the Portland Diocese, was the principal celebrant and homilist at a special anniversary Mass on December 10, 2005, to mark this historic occasion.

Today St. John's continues to play an important spiritual role with other communities of faith for citizens of Bangor and eastern Maine.

A warm welcome is extended to all visitors to come and participate at a Mass with St. John's community. The church is located at 207 York Street and is now part of the larger spiritual network of St. Paul the Apostle parish.

The original architectural rendering of St. John's Catholic Church by architect Patrick Keely is depicted here. The church was officially dedicated on October 12, 1856.

For more information, contact the parish office by telephone at (207) 942-6941, by fax at (207) 947-5984 or online at http://home.midmaine.com/-stjohnsbang.

## *Congregation Beth Israel*

There is not a great deal of historical information about Bangor Jews. There is some historical data that indicates that, prior to the Revolutionary War period, a Jewish person by either the name of Lowe or Levi may have lived in the area. The American Historical Society and authors Abraham J. Peck and Jean M. Peck of *Maine's Jewish Heritage*, published in 2007 by Arcadia Publishing, identify a Susman Abrams as having settled in the area during the period of the Revolutionary War. He conducted a tannery business in Union for many years. He died there in 1830 at the age of eighty-seven.

Prior to the 1840s, a few scattered Jewish individuals were noted as living in the area, but no Jewish community existed. As late as 1849, the Jewish population of Bangor was estimated to consist of twelve families.

Bangor during the 1840s was enjoying a major economic expansion due to its becoming the nation's largest lumber exporter. A surge in the Queen City's population occurred during the decade between 1840 and 1850, which included a large number of Irish Catholic immigrants as well as young Jews who arrived in New York from Germany, Austria and Poland. With the passing of the Yankee peddler, an economic vacuum was created, allowing these new young Jewish arrivals to fill.

Congregation Ahawas Achim was established as the first Jewish organization in Bangor in 1849. This group rented a hall for religious services and purchased a tract of land for a cemetery. It was not the destiny of these Jews to build a lasting house of worship, and by 1856, most had either moved away or had become assimilated by their gentile neighbors.

Although there were some Polish Jews among the early settlers, it was not until the 1880s that mass immigration from Eastern Europe started. When Jews from Lithuania and Poland started arriving in Bangor, they found a few German Jews already established. It soon became quite apparent that the two groups of Jews were culturally different. Within two decades, the small, older German Jewish group was totally assimilated and integrated into the burgeoning Bangor Jewish community. It is within this setting that Congregation Beth Israel was born.

"Tekiah"—when this first sound of the shofar was heard at the beginning of the High Holy Days of 1888 in Bangor, it was more than the traditional call to prayer. This year, the Tekiah heralded the formal organization of Beth Israel, the oldest active Jewish congregation in Maine.

The minyan of ten that organized the congregation more than a century ago were a robust and colorful group of young men in their twenties and early thirties who earned their living by peddling small wares from a pack.

In the fall of 1888, Bangor's small Jewish community gathered together for Rosh Hashanah. There was no rabbi or synagogue. Joe Bernstein, a cultured and scholarly man, conducted the service. One of the first acts of the fledgling congregation was to secure their own Sefer Torah and return the Torah they had on loan to Ohabei Shalom.

Over the years, the members of Congregation Beth Israel have placed great importance on having a place to pray. On August 22, 1897, the cornerstone for Congregation Beth Israel's first shul on Center Street was laid. Mr. Louis Goldberg was one of the cosigners of the first mortgage for the synagogue. Father Hennessey, a priest at St. Mary's Parish and a close personal friend of Louis Goldberg, had such admiration for the spirit for the fledging Jewish community that he personally canvassed Catholic business establishments on Exchange Street. The priest raised a considerable amount of money to aid in the construction of the synagogue. On April 30, 1911, a disastrous fire swept through Bangor, killing two people, injuring many and destroying much property, including the synagogue.

Shortly after the fire settlement with the insurance company, the Center Street lot was sold, and the present synagogue's York Street site was purchased. On October 13, 1911, a contract was awarded to the Export Company of New York to commence work on the new synagogue. On March 9, 1913, the new synagogue was dedicated. Many Bangor and state dignitaries attended this happy and solemn occasion.

From its small beginnings over 120 years ago, Congregation Beth Israel has played a significant role in keeping both the Jewish community and the city of Bangor moving ahead. On Sunday, September 7, 2008,

Congregation Beth Israel's first shul on Center Street, Bangor, was dedicated in 1897 and was destroyed in the fire of 1911.

Congregation Beth Israel celebrated its 120th anniversary as Maine's oldest Jewish house of worship. To honor this achievement, a ten-year-old idea to create an oral history of the shul, together with a forty-five-minute documentary film, was undertaken. The film depicts not only the early years of Jews in the Queen City but documents how life was for most Mainers at the turn of the nineteenth century

As a conservative synagogue, Congregation Beth Israel serves the worshipping needs of Jews in the Greater Bangor area. All are welcome to daven here. Congregation Beth Israel is located at 144 York Street. For more information, contact the synagogue by telephone at (207) 945-3433, by fax at (207) 945-3840 or visit its website at www.cbisrael.org.

## *Hammond Street Congregational Church*

In 2008, the Hammond Street Congregational Church marked its 175th anniversary as a Bangor house of worship. The Reverend John Maltby Jr. was the church's first pastor. He delivered his first sermon to about seventy-three Congregationalists from the west side of Bangor's Kenduskeag Stream. After separating from the First Congregational Church on Bangor's east side and two years of planning, raising money, selecting a site and construction, the Hammond Street Congregational Church was completed and dedicated.

Due to overrunning the $15,000 that was allocated for constructing a brick structure with a slate roof and interior meeting rooms, the original design was scaled down. Twenty years later, in 1853, sufficient money was raised to renovate the exterior, lengthen and heighten the walls and to add the single spire common to most churches. Except for the addition of the Arthur Little Wing, a century later, the Hammond Street Congregational Church looks today much as it did in the mid-1850s.

The Hammond Street Congregational Church has been added to the National Register of Historic Places. The original structure includes a large sanctuary, a choir loft with organ, a midlevel entry, bathrooms, a kitchen, a medium-sized room for meetings and classes and a large vestry. The Arthur Little Wing addition has two floors and contains offices, a parlor, a nursery, a small kitchen, two preschool daycare rooms, bathrooms, a food cupboard and storage.

During the church's 175-year history, there have been sixteen called pastors, including the church's present pastor, the Reverend Dr. Mark Allen Doty. Through the years, several associate ministers have been called to assist the pastor in supervising educational programs, visiting the ill and shut-ins, preaching and handling other church duties.

The Hammond Street Congregational Church has had a close association with the Bangor Theological Seminary, an institution whose origin precedes the church. Until several years ago, the seminary was located in close proximity to the church, and as a result, seminary leaders and faculty participated actively in the life of the church. Through the years, the church frequently hosted seminary convocations.

Hammond Street Congregational Church was dedicated circa 1898.

Christian service to the community and outreach to the world has always been a hallmark mission of the church. Today, after more than three decades, the Hammond Street Congregational Church continues to maintain its ecumenical community food pantry. It is deeply involved in supporting the Bangor Shelter, as well as continuing to support the Shaw House, a home for homeless teenagers. Once a month, the church provides free luncheons for the homeless and those in need.

On the first Sunday of the month, Communion services are held as part of the worship service. For additional church information, call (207) 942-4381 or e-mail hscc@midmaine.com.

## *Bangor Theological Seminary*

The Bangor Theological Seminary has deep historical roots in the Queen City. It was founded in the early nineteenth century, having received its charter in 1814 as a Christian seminary to train Congregational ministers to serve churches in northern New England and as missionaries around the world. It was initially named the Maine Charity School and was located on the grounds of Hamden Academy, where it remained until 1819 when it moved to its Bangor campus.

In 1820, the seminary graduated its first class of six men. Up until the late 1960s, seminary students continued to be male college graduates who wished to dedicate their life to preaching and doing God's work.

Low enrollment and financial hard times have occurred at various times during the seminary's nearly two centuries of service. Enrollment fell from nine graduates in the class of 1826 to only one graduate in the class of 1831, but in 1838, a total of fifty men were to graduate. Enrollment dipped again during the Civil War years.

Counted among the seminary's illustrious graduates are Civil War hero and later Maine governor Joshua Chamberlain and Hannibal Hamlin, who served as Abraham Lincoln's first vice president from 1861 to 1865 as well as a Maine governor and U.S. senator.

Through the years, the seminary's mission has not changed significantly. Today it is focused on training leaders, both clergy and lay, for small churches in New England and beyond. Bangor Theological Seminary currently offers academic programs leading to the master of divinity degree, the master of arts degree and the doctor of ministry degree. The seminary is ecumenical in nature with over a dozen religious traditions represented among students and faculty. It is but one of seven United Church of Christ seminaries in the United States and is the only accredited theological institution in northern New England.

A drop in full-time student enrollment placed the seminary in financial jeopardy, forcing the board to make a difficult but necessary decision in order to stay a viable institution for the future. In the fall of 2005, the Bangor Theological Seminary embarked on a new chapter in its life by moving its offices, classrooms and library from its historic Union Street campus to space on the Husson College campus. The location of these two venerable institutions allows for the sharing of resources. The seminary will continue to remain an independent, degree-granting institution.

Bangor Theology Seminary offers its students an opportunity to study religion and spirituality in a Christian context. Many different and innovative ways for individuals and groups to connect with their spirituality are available through many creative programs.

Seminary students tend to be more mature than most college students; the seminarians average in their forties, and the majority are from Maine. Bangor Theological Seminary allows students without a bachelor's degree to earn both a bachelor's and master's in five years.

Since 1991, Bangor Theological Seminary has been a school with two locations. The seminary's Portland campus provides educational opportunities for commuter students from the rapidly expanding population of southern Maine and neighboring New Hampshire and Massachusetts. Each campus is fully accredited, and degree programs may be completed solely on one campus or in a combination of studies on both campuses.

The David Nelson Beach Chapel on the original Bangor Theological Seminary Campus.

The Bangor campus is located at 2 College Circle, and the Portland campus at 159 State Street, Portland, Maine.

For additional information about the Bangor campus, call (207) 942-6781 or (800) 287-6781 or visit the website at www.bts.edu.

## *The Friars' Bakehouse*

The Franciscan Brothers of St. Elizabeth of Hungary, a Roman Catholic religious community, was founded in 1995 by Brother Donald Paul and Brother Kenneth Leo deep in the woods of Mariaville, a small rural community east of Eddington, Maine. To support themselves, the brothers started baking bread and selling it on street corners around metro Bangor. They sold bread from the back of their old Ford Bronco. Their bright school bus–yellow "Bread Ahead" signs could be found from Greater Bangor to Bar Harbor. In 2001, Brothers Donald and Kenneth opened the Friars' Bakehouse to handle their burgeoning bread business, as well as provide a spiritual destination where their customers could come and meditate, reflect and worship. The Friars' Bakehouse is located at 21 Central Street in downtown Bangor. On the first floor is the kitchen for baking and preparing meals and a dining area where one can enjoy a nourishing lunch and fellowship. Spiritual needs are met in the St. Francis and St. Claire Chapel on the second floor.

The patron saint of their order, Saint Francis of Assisi, is well known to Christians and non-Christians alike, while their patroness, Saint Elizabeth, is not as well recognized. In fact, the name Elizabeth is not found often in either the Old or New Testaments. In Hebrew, the word "El" means God, and Elizabeth "God in the fullness." In the New Testament, we find Elizabeth, mother of John the Baptist and a relative of Mary and Jesus, who is mentioned several times in Luke's Gospel.

Saint Elizabeth, patroness of their order, was born in 1207 to King Andrew II of Hungary and his wife, Gertrude. Although Elizabeth was raised in the castle of Warburg that provided all the pomp and wealth one would expect from court life of that period, she grew up a very religious child. Her spiritual growth continued to flourish as she matured. Perhaps she was influenced by her lifetime experiences, which included the murder of her mother in 1213 by a group of Hungarian nobles, along with the abusive treatment she received from the more secularly centered Thuringia court where she lived after being betrothed to Hermann I's eldest son. Upon that son's death, Elizabeth was betrothed to his younger brother, Louis. In 1221, the two were married. Louis and Elizabeth had an exemplary marriage, and Louis supported his wife's charitable works against the will of the court. The couple had three children, a son and two daughters. In 1226, a major flood, famine and pests brought havoc to Thuringia. During this period, Elizabeth provided daily aid to hundreds. This segment of Elizabeth's life is a major factor of why she is remembered. The following year, her husband, Louis, was killed while on a crusade to the Holy Land.

After becoming a widow, Elizabeth consecrated her life to Christ and formally renounced the world, as she accepted the habit of the Third Order of St. Francis of Assisi. Shortly after her death, healing miracles were reported at her grave and at the church of the hospital that she had started. She was canonized on Pentecost Sunday in 1235. The inclusion of St. Elizabeth in their order's name signifies their view of the importance of both sexes in God's work.

Brothers Donald and Kenneth are dedicated to their vows to follow Christ and to their apostolate to serve. Every loaf of bread baked helps fulfill their calling. They serve that need as Christ commanded both locally and globally. In the city of Bangor, they were able to coordinate, through a network of churches, the establishment of free meals every Saturday for those in need. Their work has resulted in the Congregationalists, Methodists and Episcopalians adopting a free Saturday meal program to augment the fourth Saturday free meal program that had been established by the good people at the Unitarian Universalist Church.

On the global level, they have made numerous pilgrimages to help both the poor in Isla Mujeres, Mexico, and Cape Haitian, Haiti.

Currently the brothers are completing work on their newly established retreat house on a thirty-four-acre parcel of property in Bucksport, Maine. The grounds offer a memorial prayer path with meditations on the Stations of the Cross. Quiet and solitude will be the key aspect to a retreat experience. No motorized vehicles, cellphones or electronic devices are allowed on the site. The brothers' new friary is now open for retreats.

Spiritual needs of the Friars' Bakehouse customers are met in the St. Francis and St. Claire Chapel on the second floor of the bake house located at 21 Central Street in downtown Bangor.

Brothers Donald and Kenneth welcome you to come to the Friars' Bakehouse and to participate in services in their chapel.

St. Elizabeth Friary, at 1160 North Main Street, in Brewer, Maine, is the home of the brothers. During the summer months, weekly masses are often held in the friary's air-conditioned chapel. Check for times by calling (207) 947-3770.

## *First Baptist Church*

In 1818, when the First Baptist Church in Bangor was founded, Bangor was essentially a frontier settlement of the commonwealth of Massachusetts. While several buildings existed at the time on Main Street, Bangor's major settlement could be found on Broad Street near the mouth of the Kenduskeag Stream.

From colonial days to the early nineteenth century, the Congregational Church had been the official religion of Massachusetts, and under commonwealth law, everyone was required to pay a church tax to support the state religion. Six years prior to the founding of the First Baptist

Church and a little over two decades from the incorporation of Bangor by statute of the General Court of Massachusetts, a Congregational meetinghouse had been established with the Reverend Loomis as pastor.

A few Baptist families lived in the Bangor area for some years prior to the establishment of a church. In those early days, the Reverend Isaac Case of Readfield, a Baptist circuit rider, helped to keep the Baptist conviction alive by meeting on occasion in the homes of these families in what was known as "cottage prayer meetings" or "kitchen prayer meetings."

On the evening of January 30, 1818, a group gathered at the home of Thomas Bradbury on Harlow Street to organize a Baptist Church. Elders from several Baptist Churches in the region attended to conduct the initiatory services. Following a profession of faith, the group joined hands and repeated after Elder Isaac Case the Baptist Covenant. They were then declared an organized church with the name "First Baptist Church in Bangor."

Following the solemn ceremony of church organization, a man stepped forward from the shadows of the room and expressed a desire to become a church member. It was not known how this man had come to be there. He identified himself as Nathaniel Fiske. He was accordingly warmly welcomed by the group, and they then voted to accept him as a member as soon as he was baptized. The following day, Sunday January 31, 1818, Nathaniel Fiske was immersed in the icy waters of Kenduskeag Stream and baptized.

Over the first eleven years in the life of this fledging church, worship services took place in members' homes, various schools and, on occasion, in the county courthouse. Visiting missionaries and preaching circuit riders provided for the spiritual needs of the church, except for two years when they had a settled minister to lead them.

A decade after the establishment of the church, religious enthusiasm was running high, and it was decided that it was time to build a permanent house of worship. A building site was secured at the corner of Harlow and Center Streets. They also decided it was appropriate to form the Baptist Society as distinct from the First Baptist Church to separate financial matters from the spiritual. In 1828, the Reverend Thomas B. Ripley was called to be pastor during this exciting period in the church's life.

On April 16, 1829, the new building was officially dedicated as the First Baptist Church in Bangor's permanent home. Friends from Boston provided this new beautiful temple to God with a number of gifts, including a Paul Revere bell. On the lower side of the building on the Harlow Street side, there were basement store spaces that were rented to selected merchants. The income received from the rent was used to support the church.

From its very beginnings, the church possessed a great appreciation for fine music. In 1829, Mr. Hoit was employed to improve the music of the church. It was not until 1835 that the first organ was installed in the church. It was purchased for $1,000 and served the church for thirty years.

The Great Bangor Fire of April 30, 1911, destroyed the First Baptist Church, as well as many houses of worship in the Queen City. On June 15, 1913, a new place was dedicated. The new church building and site cost about $55,000. The main floor of the new church building consists of an auditorium and conference room that can be reached by either the main or rear entrances. Lobbies are found both to the right and left of the pulpit, and the baptistery is located behind it. The Communion table that was saved from the fire was incorporated into the new house of worship's spiritual life. A beautiful Tiffany stained glass window depicting the Ascension was given to the Church as a memorial to Mr. and Mrs. Arad Thompson by their daughters. A magnificent new pipe organ assured that the church's appreciation for sacred music would be sustained. The vestries were located below the main floor, as was the Bible School Assembly room. The library, classroom space, church parlor, kitchen, restrooms and boiler room were also housed in this area. Over the main entrance was located the pastor's study. In the tower of the new church was a splendid Meneely Bell, weighing 1,562 pounds and bearing the inscription on its rim of "God's in his Heaven, all's right with the world."

In 1958, the Betterly Chapel addition was completed, and in 1988, the Carrie Rowe Educational Wing was added to the facility. A lift and ramp to provide handicap accessibility in 1991 completed modern updates to the church.

The First Baptist Church is located at 56 Center Street and is affiliated with American Baptist Churches USA. For additional information, contact the church by telephone at (207) 945-9694 or via e-mail at churchoffice@fbcbangor.org.

The First Baptist Church, Bangor, was dedicated on April 16, 1829.

## *St. John's Episcopal Church*

The Episcopal Church of Maine's roots date back to 1605 when a Church of England prayer service was conducted on Monhegan Island off the coast of Maine by the explorer George Weymouth. When he took possession of this rocky island, he erected a discoverer's cross for the Church of England on a high point of the island. Two years later, on August 9, 1607, the Reverend Richard Seymore, a member of an English expedition, held the first Thanksgiving service in what is present-day Maine on St. Georges Island before landing at the mouth of the Kennebec River. Thus rites of the Episcopal Church were conducted here in Maine thirteen years before the Pilgrims landed at Plymouth Rock.

At the time of the American Revolution, the Episcopal Church was struggling to establish itself here as a new church based on the solid foundation of the Anglican Church. The politics and conflict of the Revolution nearly destroyed the fledging Episcopal Church. Calm only returned after all Tory priests had gone to Canada or returned to England. At the war's end, there were no Anglican priests in Maine.

In 1810, the Eastern Diocese of the Episcopal Church was established. It included Massachusetts, Rhode Island, New Hampshire, Vermont and present-day Maine, which was part of the commonwealth of Massachusetts until 1820. Twenty parishes made up the new Eastern Diocese. While the church was established in Maine, it was not until 1834 that its presence was made in Bangor.

In 1834, Bangor residents Charles Hayes, Adolphus Converse, Joseph Bryant and Jonathan Young began the process of organizing an Episcopal parish in Bangor. Charles Hayes was chosen to chair a building committee in 1835 and, according to ledger records, selected architect Richard Upjohn to design their church. After arriving in Bangor from England in 1830, Upjohn designed several important homes in the Queen City, including the Isaac Farrar Mansion and the Thomas A. Hill House. It is believed that through these architectural projects he became known to Charles Hayes and the building committee. After designing St. John's Church in Bangor, Upjohn went on to become a prominent American architect with a specialty in ecclesiological Gothic Revival churches and founder of the American Institute of Architects.

The first St. John's Church was built of wood in a Gothic Revival style during the years 1835 and 1836. It was consecrated in 1839 after its debts were settled. The Right Reverend Alexander Viets Griswold, bishop of the Eastern Diocese, officiated at the consecration. The *Diocesan Journal* of 1840, according to Harris Walter Reynolds in his *The Beginnings of St. John's Church*, listed church membership of 50 families and 34 communicants. By 1884, church membership had grown to 109 families, 207 communicants and Sunday school enrollment of 101.

The Easter fire of 1911 that swept through Bangor completely destroyed St. John's Church, as well as several other houses of worship. Replacement planning began almost at once. The building committee was comprised of the Reverend Walter Lott, Franklin Carlton and Percy R. Todd. They selected the grandson of Richard Upjohn, Hobart B. Upjohn of the New York architectural firm of Upjohn and Conable, to design a stone replica of the first church.

The new church building is actually of frame construction and the interior detailing of wood and plaster. The interior finishing was laborious and very expensive. The cement molds for the cluster columns were made in the church, and the plastering of interior surfaces took over four months in 1913. Due to mounting costs, the planned spire and projecting choir room were omitted from the project. Two objects that were saved from the burning church were the lectern and marble baptismal font. They were installed in the new church and are still in use today.

The entire new church was reopened on February 10, 1918. During construction, the completed basement vestry room served for parish worship services for four years. The mortgage for this expensive construction project was paid off in 1926, and on June 20 of that year, the Right Reverend Benjamin Brewster formally dedicated the new St. John's Church.

In 1939, the women of the parish financed the construction of the parish house and Bethlehem Chapel. Brewer architect Edwin S. Kent designed the Bethlehem Chapel to be architecturally in harmony with the stone Gothic structure of the church. All of the stained glass memorial windows in both buildings were designed by Charles J. Connick Associates of Boston and were installed over a period of years.

The grandson of Richard Upjohn, who designed the first St. John's Episcopal Church that was destroyed in the Great Bangor Fire of 1911, was selected to design a stone replica of that first church. The new church was formally dedicated on June 20, 1926.

The parish house, which is the link between the church and chapel, was totally remodeled in 1995 to provide for a handicapped-accessible entrance, an elevator and a functional space for meetings and the choir. A few years prior to these enhancements, the parish purchased a home at 234 French Street from Husson College. This facility serves as the parish office, as well as providing for additional meeting space.

St. John's Episcopal Church is located at 225 French Street. For additional information, contact the church by telephone at (207) 947-0156 or visit the website at www.stjohnbangor.org.

### *St. George Greek Orthodox Church*

St. George Greek Orthodox Church in Bangor is a beacon of orthodoxy in the most northeastern corner of the United States. Although it is one of the smaller churches in the Boston metropolis, it serves one of the largest geographical areas.

George N. Brountas, a remarkable young man from the small mountain village of Vamvakou, Greece, immigrated to America in order to help his family. After a brief stay in Boston, he settled in Bangor in 1897 and became the first person of the Orthodox faith in Bangor. Initially, he sold fruit from a pushcart that he pushed from Bangor to Orono. George's solitary pushcart venture ended when he started a new business; the Bangor Candy Kitchen. As his new business grew, he was able to bring his father and siblings to America. His four siblings stayed in the Bangor area and married and raised families. After a stay in the area, his father returned to his homeland. Over time, many others from Vamvakou came and settled in Bangor.

In 1905, the three Zoidis brothers—Gregor, Nicholas and Apostlos—arrived from Epirus, a small hamlet near the Greek-Albanian border. The brothers were followed by family members and friends from their homeland. Like their Greek brothers, their greatest strength was their faith. As the community grew, a priest was summoned several times a year to perform the divine liturgy and to administer the sacraments. The first visiting priest was the Reverend Esihios Raptakis from Biddeford, Maine. A church organization was formed on November 11, 1923, and a petition for a parish charter was sent to the Greek Orthodox Archdiocese of North and South America. The fledging Bangor Orthodox community received their first full-time priest, the Reverend Haralambos Economakos, in December 1923. Initially, services were held at the Royal Arcanum Hall on Exchange

Street but were later moved to the Ancient Order of Hibernians Hall on the corner of Union and Main Streets. A choir, Greek school and adult religious instruction classes were soon initiated.

On May 22, 1926, fifty members of the community pledged $1,200 and organized to form the Saint George Orthodox Community of Bangor. The corporation was accredited by the state of Maine in July. In 1929, the Reverend Polycarp Marinakis arrived as pastor of the Bangor community. He soon initiated the idea of a church structure. The church was to be named in honor of the patron saint of three contributing donors, as recommended by George J. Limberis. These donors were George N. Brountas, George Floros and George Skoufis. In November 1929, construction was started on the new church. The structure was to be ninety by forty feet and not pretentious but modern and comfortable. The plans called for a vestry, Sunday school rooms and an auditorium.

The Right Reverend Bishop Joachim Alexopoulos, assisted by Reverend Cyril Gregory of Portland and the Reverend Polycarp Marinakis, dedicated the new church with the ancient consecration rites

St. George Greek Orthodox Church on Sanford Street, Bangor, was dedicated on September 7, 1930, by the Right Reverend Bishop Joachim Alexopoulos with the ancient consecration rites.

on September 7, 1930. The bishop told the congregation gathered for the dedication of the noble tradition and great religious heritage of the Greek Church and urged its followers to carry on the torch of God and the heritage and faith of their forefathers. To the community, the church was a fulfillment of a vision and the culmination of years of planning and a true symbol of their faith.

Through the years, many improvements to the church have been undertaken. In December 1961, the present rectory at 252 Fourteenth Street was purchased. St. George Greek Orthodox Church is located at 90 Sanford Street.

For additional church information, contact the rectory at (207) 945-9588.

## *St. Mary's Catholic Church*

In 1769, Seth Buswell arrived in present-day Bangor and built a log cabin on what was to become Newbury Street. This new frontier was called Kenduskeag Plantation until 1791, when the General Court of Massachusetts granted it incorporation as Bangor.

Twenty-eight years after Seth Buswell had settled in the area, the Reverend Jean Louis Lefebvre Cheverus made his first missionary visit to the Penobscot Indians. He stopped at Seth Buswell's overnight and preached that day in front of Seth's home. During this visit, Father Cheverus celebrated the first Mass to be recorded in Bangor. By 1800, the population of Bangor had risen to three hundred. A few of these new residents of the Queen City were Catholic.

In 1825, Bishop Fenwick came from Boston to visit and preach in Bangor. At that time, the priests who were caring for the spiritual needs of the Penobscot Indians at Old Town would on occasion visit the few Catholics in Bangor.

During those early years, Mass would be celebrated on occasion in the homes of local Bangor Catholics. It's recorded that Father James Conway, who was a missionary to the Penobscot Indians in Old Town, celebrated Mass at the home of James Carr on Court Street and at another private home on Broad Street.

In the early 1830s, Irish immigrants started arriving in Bangor to work in the fledging lumber industry. In 1832, Bishop Fenwick wrote that Bangor was destined to become one of the first cities of America, and there was no other place in his diocese he so much desired to found a church.

In 1830, the Reverend Virgil Barber witnessed the marriage of Thomas Cooney and Mary Scott on Indian Island, Old Town. The Indian Island mission was the only Catholic site along the Penobscot River for Mass and sacraments. Two years later, this couple had a son, who was then baptized by Father Barber. This was the first recording of a baptism of a white child in the region.

Father Patrick McNamee, a cousin of Thomas Cooney, became a permanent resident of Bangor in 1832. The following spring a lot was purchased for a church, and Father McNamee became the first resident pastor and was to begin building. Things did not go too smoothly, and in 1835, Father Michael Lynch took charge of the Bangor mission. That summer, ground was broken for Bangor's first Catholic Church on Court Street. St. Michael's was dedicated the following winter.

In 1853, the Reverend John Baptst, S.J., was placed in charge of all missions in Maine east of the Penobscot River, with Bangor to serve as his residency. At that time, the Catholic population o f Bangor had swelled to six thousand, and it was apparent that a larger church was required. The cornerstone for Bangor's second Catholic Church, St. John's, was laid in its present location on York Street in 1855.

During the last third of the nineteenth century, the Catholic population continued to grow within the Greater Bangor area, and in May 1872, Bangor's congregation was divided into two parishes: St. John's and St. Mary's. The Reverend James W. Murphy was appointed as pastor of the new St. Mary's parish.

Father Murphy was assigned the task of building a new church, as well as caring for the spiritual needs of a congregation that covered an area of Bangor west of Kenduskeag Stream, Hampden, Hermon and Carmel. Land that had previously served as a gravel pit on Cedar Street was purchased for $2,000 together with two adjacent lots that cost approximately $1,000 each. This acquired land at the corner of Cedar and First Streets would become the site for St. Mary's Church.

In September 1872 the cornerstone for St. Mary's was laid by Bishop D.W. Bacon of Portland. During the construction period, Bangor's City Hall auditorium was used as a place of worship. Masses were held there for a little more than a year. On completion of the basement for the new church, a temporary altar and seating were installed, and Mass was held there until the new church was completed. On December 8, 1874, the Right Reverend Bishop Lynch of Charleston, South Carolina, delivered the dedication oration.

It is not known when the joyous bells of St. Mary's first tolled, echoing from rooftops and tree tops and ever ascending through space and time in grateful thanks for God's great gifts.

During the 1880s, Father Michael C. O'Brien, an able administrator and pastor, built a rectory at the corner of Main and Cedar Streets, as well as a school and convent on First Street. He was also responsible for bringing the Sisters of Mercy and Christian Brothers to teach in the new parochial school.

Through the years, St. Mary's was blessed with many able pastors and assistants who provided devoted stewardship to the congregation. A number of projects on the church property in the interest of appropriate maintenance were undertaken. During the early 1950s, Monsignor Edward F. Ward, as pastor of St. Mary's, formed a lay committee to plan and implement a major reconstruction of the church building. The implemented plan not only addressed structural repairs but also included redecorating and refurnishing the entire interior of the church and bringing the entire ninety-year-old building in compliance with existing building codes.

On the weekend of October 20–22, 1972, St. Mary's opened its centennial celebrations. On Friday evening of October 20, a concelebrated Mass was offered by Bishop Peter L. Gerety and fourteen priests who had served in the parish.

In 1980, a new modern St. Mary's Church was completed on its campus site on Ohio Street. The first Mass celebrated in the new house of worship was on All Saints' Day. In addition to the new church, the campus houses a rectory and All Saints St. Mary's Campus facility for grades kindergarten through three.

St. Mary's is located at 768 Ohio Street, is in Deanery IV for Southern Penobscot, Hancock and Waldo Counties and is a member of Cluster 9 and St. Paul the Apostle Parish. For additional information, contact the church by telephone at (207) 945-5018 or via e-mail at stmarysbangor@roadrunner.com.

St. Mary's Catholic Church has served its parishoners for nearly 140 years. The new modern church shown here was completed on its campus site in 1980.

## *Redeemer Lutheran Church, ELCA*

In 1959, Bangor had thirty-five churches representing almost every major denomination—except Lutheran. At that time, Dow Air Force Base (now Bangor International Airport) was in full operation, and a Lutheran chaplain, Captain Norman G. Folkers, was stationed on the base to provide for the spiritual needs of service personnel stationed there. Chaplain Folkers was conducting the Protestant services at the base three Sundays of each month and a Lutheran communion service on the first Sunday of the month. These services were open to civilians and military personnel, and Chaplain Folkers attempted to serve as pastor to all who were interested in the Lutheran faith. At that time, there were approximately forty Lutheran students enrolled at the University of Maine in Orono, as well as the university's faculty members, students at Husson College and Lutheran families scattered throughout the Greater Bangor area. The need for a Lutheran Church in Bangor was apparent. Chaplain Folkers was very eager to see one established and was dedicated to doing everything possible to assist a Lutheran body coming into the Bangor area.

On December 7, 1960, a group of eighty-five enthusiastic people gathered at the *Bangor Daily News* auditorium for a meeting to form a Lutheran Church in Bangor. An informal committee consisting of Major Melvin Saager, Dr. Marie Mengers and Mr. Carrol Hall were appointed to arrange for a place to worship. The First Methodist Church on Pine Street, Bangor, invited the fledging Lutheran body to use their facilities for worship services. The first service was held on December 28, with eighty-five people present. A schedule for ongoing services was arranged with a committee from the Methodist Church. It was decided that the newly formed Lutheran body could use the Methodist Church facilities on Sunday afternoons, and the official first service would be held at 2:00 p.m. on February 19, 1961. The Reverend Carl A. Bergquist and his family arrived from Waltham, Massachusetts, and proceeded to get settled.

At the new church's historic first formal worship, Dr. Eskil Englund of the New England Conference commissioned Pastor Berquist as board missionary. More than 100 were present for this service. On June 4, 1961, the Redeemer Evangelical Lutheran Church of Bangor, Maine, was formerly organized and incorporated with a charter membership of 101 adults and 89 children, making a total baptized membership of 190.

On January 25, 1962, final papers were passed, and the 2.9-acre land package on Essex Street, which was known as the "old Arsenal property," became the site for the new Redeemer Lutheran Church of Bangor. A true beating of swords into plowshare transformation took place with this historic land transfer. A century earlier, on the morning of May 14, 1861, 2,700 men of the Second Maine Regiment marched away from their base here at the Bangor State Arsenal to serve the north in the Civil War.

The new Redeemer Lutheran Church has a modern brick exterior construction and was built at a cost of $75,000. The church altar is of marble chip and epoxy paneling, and the church has as its focal point

The newly formed Redeemer Lutheran Church of Bangor held its first service on December 28, 1960, at the First Methodist Church on Pine Street, Bangor.

a thirty-two-foot free-standing cross that is lighted at night. Formal dedication of the new church home took place on May 16, 1965.

The year 1968 saw the closing of Dow Air Force Base, and this event resulted in a short-term steep decrease in the church's membership. Over the next four decades, Redeemer Lutheran Church experienced significant growth in its membership.

Redeemer Lutheran Church is located at 540 Essex Street. For additional information, contact the church by telephone at (207) 945-3166 or online at redeemer-lutheran-church.org.

### *Congregation Beth El*

In the spring of 1981, Congregation Beth El was born in Bangor as the region's only Reform synagogue. An earlier Beth El had existed some forty years earlier, but it had been subsumed under Congregation Beth Israel, and its Reform identity had been lost. The Congregation Beth El development process began when several families of the area placed an advertisement in the *Jewish Community Council Newsletter* announcing an open meeting. This announcement created a great response, and within a short time, twenty-five families had initiated the development of a Reform synagogue.

The fledging Beth El initially scheduled its worship services on one Friday a month. These services were held alternatively in the Jewish Community Center and the Unitarian Universalist Church and were led by congregation members.

It became apparent early in the life of Beth El that some basic decisions, such as where services should be held and whether there should be a religious school, as well as who would teach the children, needed to be made. Other important issues needing to be resolved included whether the laws of Kashruth should be strictly observed for the Onegs and how would the congregation handle its financial requirements.

Over a short period of time, the congregation addressed these issues and began to develop its own identity and traditions, as well as increase its membership. Members from the Acadia and Way Down East regions and the Katahdin area, as well as Greater Bangor, were soon a vital part of Beth El spiritual life.

By 1983, there were thirteen students enrolled in the religious school, studying Jewish history, Hebrew and Jewish holiday traditions. Beth El had its first B'nai Mitzvah in October 1983. Through the mid-1980s, Beth El enjoyed having a visiting rabbi for services. For the High Holy Days starting in 1982, Rabbi Paul Menitoff traveled with his family from Boston to Bangor for these services. Since Beth El did not have a Torah, Rabbi Menitoff brought a borrowed Torah with him for use during the services.

A significant milestone was achieved when Beth El received its membership in the UAHC. It also was blessed with the presentation of a two-hundred-year-old Torah that had been rescued from Czechoslovakia after World War II and had been fully restored by the Westminster Synagogue Trust in London. This Torah had been designated to be loaned for use by young congregations until they could afford to buy a Torah of their own.

In 1987, David Sandmel assumed the position of rabbi on a part-time basis while sharing his time with a sister Reform Congregation in Portland. Within a year, Rabbi Sandmel needed to devote his full-time duties to the Portland congregation. Rabbi Shoshana Perry was enlisted to serve part time. During the next several years, she would travel two long weekends per month from New York City and later from Philadelphia while finishing school to serve Beth El. In 1991, Rabbi Perry moved to Bangor to become Congregation Beth El's first resident rabbi. She served in that role until 1994, when she accepted a position in a larger Boston-area synagogue.

A search committee was established in 1994 to select a full-time replacement for Rabbi Perry. After a comprehensive search, Rabbi Laurence Elis Milder was selected to be the spiritual leader of Congregation Beth El. The following year, the congregation purchased a building at 183 French Street, which had served as the Messiah Baptist Church, as the new permanent home for Congregation Beth El. On a cold and snowy March 1, Rabbi Milder and congregants proudly walked the Torah from the Unitarian Universalist Church to its new synagogue. In April, with many dignitaries, including the governor, in attendance, Congregation Beth El was officially dedicated.

A generous donation of land abutting other Jewish cemeteries near Bangor's Mount Hope Cemetery was given by Congregation Beth Israel to Beth El in 2002. These sacred grounds will serve the needs of Beth El members for many years to come.

In April 1995, Congregation Beth El's new spiritual home on French Street, Bangor, was officially dedicated.

In 2005, Rabbi Milder, after serving Congregation Beth El for over a decade, took a new position with a larger congregation in Westborough, Massachusetts. Beth El's search committee, after interviewing a number of applicants, selected Darah Lerner for its new spiritual leader.

Congregation Beth El continues to thrive with friendliness, warmth and a welcoming spirit to newcomers and support through *simchas* and grief. Beth El has developed a strong tradition of social activism, which is expressed through social action, education and worship. As part of Congregation Beth El's twenty-fifth-anniversary celebration, major renovations to the synagogue were completed in 2008. The growing congregation stands as a powerful Jewish voice in Bangor and eastern Maine, as it continues to move forward toward its vision for 2015.

For additional information, contact Congregation Beth El by telephone at (207) 945-4578 or via e-mail at bethel@me.acadia.net.

## Winterport

### *St. Gabriel's Catholic Church*

The Waldo County town of Winterport is situated on the west bank of the Penobscot River. Early settlement dates from 1766, and the town called Frankfort, which included the region that is now Winterport, was incorporated in 1799. It was not until 1860 that Winterport became a separate town.

Few immigrants of the Catholic faith settled in Winterport before the tide of Irish immigration entered the Greater Bangor area during the 1840s. The Maine and New Hampshire Granite Company and the firm of Pierce and Rowe had opened granite quarries on Musketon and Waldo Mountains to supply stone for its growing demand in Boston, New York and Philadelphia for buildings, roads and bridges. The hardy Irishmen, fleeing from the famine at home, were delighted by the prospects of an honest livelihood here in Winterport, Maine.

During the early period of influx of Irish Catholics to Winterport, their spiritual needs were occasionally met by visits by Fathers T. O'Sullivan and Moore of Bangor. On these visits, Mass was celebrated in the homes of Thomas Morrissey and Thomas McDonough and in David McDermott's new barn.

James Reilly, an Irishman from County Meath, settled in Winterport in 1839. In January 1850, Mary Haley from County Sligo arrived in Winterport. She and James Reilly met and were soon married. After establishing their home in town, they made it the spiritual location for celebrating Mass when Jesuit mission priests Fathers Necker, Force, Chiampi and Bapst visited their community.

It was with this family that Father Bapst sought refuge from the trying experience he suffered at the hands of a Know-Nothing mob in Ellsworth. Father Bapst told his hosts little of his trials by that mob but was not reticent in expressing his appreciation for the noble stand taken by some non-Catholic men of Bangor, who called together the best citizens of the Queen City in an indignation meeting to condemn the insults and violence of the Ellsworth mob. These honorable non-Catholic gentlemen not only demonstrated their principles of toleration and fair play but also presented Father Bapst with a valuable gold watch as a token of their respect.

In 1853, Fathers Bapst and Chiampi secured a lot from the Sproul Estate in the lower village of Winterport to serve as the site for a church. Building operations were started in the fall, and in the following year, the church was occupied and the first Mass was celebrated in the little sanctuary overlooking the Penobscot. Father Bapst presented the church with a valuable copy of Raphael's *Madonna of the Chair*, which he hung above the high altar.

During this period, the Diocese of Portland was established. Father Bapst's next big challenge was to build St. John's Church in Bangor. The cornerstone for St. John's was laid on December 8, 1854. While engaged in this monumental task, several different priests visited the Mission of St. Gabriel's in Winterport over a seven-year period, including the Reverends Vinton Linto, John Murphy, Eugene Vetromile, Michael Gallagher and Cullen.

In 1862, a new parish was formed by Bishop Bacon with a resident pastor at Ellsworth. Winterport was detached from the Bangor parish whose fortunes it had shared from the beginning and was placed in the Ellsworth group of outlying missions.

St. Gabriel's Catholic Church was established in 1850. The photo depicts the new parish in the 1850s.

In the summer of 1876, St Gabriel's was dedicated by Bishop James A. Healy, and the Reverend Jerimiah McCarthy was appointed as its first resident pastor. St. Gabriel's was also made the seat of a parish at this time with missions at Bucksport, Frankfort, Searsport and Belfast.

St. Gabriel's Church has served the spiritual needs of Winterport Catholics for more than 150 years. The church is part of Cluster 9 and Deanery IV, which serves Southern Penobscot, Hancock and Waldo Counties. St. Gabriel's Church is also a member of St. Paul the Apostle Parish.

St. Gabriel's Church is located on lower Main Street. For additional information, call (207) 862-3517 or e-mail gabmat@tds.net.

## BREWER

### *First Congregational Church, UCC*

From about 1786, the sparsely settled town of Brewer and the surrounding towns of Orrington and Holden were on occasion provided religious services by the Reverend Seth Noble. He ministered at that time to both the communities of Bangor and Brewer and received an annual salary of $400, which the two communities shared. In the summer of 1800, several leading members of the Brewer community met to form a permanent church on the banks of the Penobscot River. The group included Colonel and Mrs. John Brewer, Deacon Robinson and Dr. Elisha Skinner.

On September 9, 1800, the church was incorporated, and a Mr. James Boyd was examined by the founding church group and found fit to serve as their first minister. Shortly after the church's organization, a covenant and Articles of Faith were written. A profession of faith based upon these articles became the process by which one became a member of the church.

The Civil War era of 1861 to 1865 saw many young men of the congregation go off to serve as Union soldiers. Many other members of the congregation were actively involved in the abolitionist movement. Several members were directly involved in the Underground Railroad, with specific safe houses being provided by Oliver Farrington and Deacon John Holyoke. The most well-known member of the First Congregational Church of Brewer associated with this period of American history was Joshua L. Chamberlain. After graduating from Bowdoin College in 1852, he studied for three years at Bangor Theology Seminary and then returned to Bowdoin to begin a career in education. Although not trained in military science, Chamberlain felt a strong desire to serve his country after the outbreak of the Civil War. He left his teaching post and joined the Twentieth Maine Regiment as a lieutenant colonel. In June 1863, he was promoted to the rank of colonel. At the Battle of Gettysburg, Chamberlain achieved his fame for his valiant defense of Little Round Top. For his gallantry he received the Medal of Honor. In April 1864, he was promoted to the rank of brigadier general. After the war, he entered politics and served as governor of Maine. Upon leaving the governorship, he returned to Bowdoin to serve as a faculty member and president.

By 1879, the church building had become too small for its growing congregation, and it was cut in half in order for it to be moved to the foot of Church Street and be refurbished as two apartments. This move made it possible to construct the present church. The new house of worship was erected by Albert A. Kenny and was officially dedicated on March 28, 1890. Tiffany stained glass windows greatly enhanced the beauty of the new building. Through the years many improvements and renovations have been made to the facility, including the installation of cathedral chimes in 1935.

Due to the church's proximity to Bangor Theological Seminary, many of its Congregational students have worshipped at the church and participated in many of the church's activities. A theology student from England, Frederick C. Oliver, organized Brewer Congregational Scouts in 1908. When the Boy Scouts of America was organized in 1910, this group became affiliated with the fledging American organization as Troop One and is the first Boy Scout troop in the United States.

The First Congregational Church of Brewer joined the United Church of Christ after its formation in 1957. The church supports both national and international mission efforts of the United Church of Christ, as well as being involved in many local community endeavors, including the Brewer Community Service Council, the Brewer Christian Food

First Congregational Church, UCC, Brewer's original meetinghouse circa 1812.

Cupboard and serving dinners at the Salvation Army and the Bangor Area Homeless Shelter.

The United Church of Christ slogan—"No matter who you are and where you are on your journey, you are welcome here"—is heartfelt in the Brewer church community. The First Congregational Church, UCC, of Brewer is located at 35 Church Street. For additional information, contact the church by telephone at (207) 989-7350.

### *St. Teresa's Church*

For many years prior to 1896, the Catholics that lived in the South Brewer area were parishioners of St. John's Church in Bangor. While some of the more affluent Brewer Catholics had a carriage or cart to take them to St. John's for Mass on Sunday, most traveled the distance on foot. In September 1890, an electric-car service between Brewer and Bangor was initiated that made the travel much easier.

Monsignor Edward McSweeney, pastor of St. John's Church in Bangor, initiated in 1894 the building of St. Teresa's Church in South Brewer. A contractor was hired to supervise the construction project, which was accomplished by the willing hands of many of the future parishioners of St. Teresa's Church. Initially the basement was used for services. When the upper church was completed, the basement was adapted into a parish hall. The first Mass was celebrated in the new church by the Reverend James O'Brian.

The parish was officially formed on November 10, 1896, under the patronage of St. Teresa of Avila and was dedicated by Bishop Healy of the Portland Diocese. The Reverend Hamakers became the first resident pastor. At that time there were fewer than one hundred Catholic families in South Brewer.

In July 1915, the Reverend Matthew Reilly was appointed as pastor of St. Teresa's Church. During his pastorate, St. Teresa's School and rectory were built.

In 1922, the Sisters of Mercy arrived to teach at the new school. The original rectory became the convent for the sisters. The Sisters of Mercy taught at St. Teresa's School through 1969. In their years of service, the sisters made an important contribution to both the parish and community.

On November 6, 1945, a fire completely destroyed St. Teresa's Church. Father Maurice Carroll, the pastor, together with all the parishioners, was devastated by the loss of their church. The magnitude of this loss was further reflected by the many expressions of sympathy that were received from far and wide.

The building of a new church began on April 23, 1946, directly across the street from the site of the disastrous fire. With the untiring zeal of Father Carroll, and the support of the parishioners and the generous assistance from those outside the parish, the new and present-day St. Teresa's Church was achieved. Father Carroll remained as pastor until his death in 1951.

To comply with the decree of Vatican II, major renovations were undertaken in 1976. The following year, the Sisters of Mercy returned to St. Teresa's in the presence of Sister Catherine Green, who was hired as a religious education coordinator.

Since its founding, St. Teresa's has had a steady growth of parishioners. According to the most recent census, more than five hundred families are members of the parish.

During 1987, St. Teresa's School building was sold to Civil Engineering Services, Inc., and a fundraising program was begun to build a new parish center on the site of the original church next to the rectory. The parish center was completed and dedicated on June 4, 1994, at a cost of over $600,000. By the spring of 1995, both the parish center debt and debt from major church renovations in 1985 were totally paid off. A refurbishing of the church interior was undertaken during the summer of 1996 in preparation for the centennial celebrations.

As part of its Social Justice and Peace Commission focus, St. Teresa's became a covenant church for Habitat for Humanity.

St. Teresa's Church is a member of Deanery IV, comprising Southern Penobscot, Hancock and Waldo Counties, and in Cluster 9, as well as a member of St. Paul the Apostle Parish. St. Teresa's is located at 440 Main Street. For additional church information, contact the church office by telephone at (207) 989-6129 or via e-mail at stteresa@midmaine.com.

## EDDINGTON

### *East Eddington Community Church*

Eddington lies on the eastern bank of the Penobscot about five miles east northeast of Bangor. It is on the Air Line route east to Calais in Washington County. Bradley bounds it on the north, Clifton on the east, Holden on the south and Veazie and Orono on the west, separated by the Penobscot River.

In the early years, several villages were settled within the Eddington area. A settlement near the beautiful lake that was named for the area's first settler, Captain Samuel Davis, was originally known as Pond Village. To its west a larger village, then known as Bend Village, had been settled. In about 1816, the Universalists of Holden and Eddington built a church on the top of a hill in Bend Village for its growing population. Captain Davis was one of the new church's parishioners. He and others would travel by foot, horseback or wagon to worship there.

During the period of 1841to 1842, the parishioners of the Bend Village Church from East Eddington decided to break away from the church and form what they called the East Eddington Meetinghouse Society. John Comins and others are quoted as saying, "We are going to have a church at this time."

The new meetinghouse was built out of an old store during 1842 and 1843 and was dedicated in 1844. Elijah Comins bought the first pew (No. 18) for $37.50 and was appointed agent for sale of the remaining pews. Right Stockwell became treasurer for the fledging church, and the Reverend Jerome Harris became the first pastor of the East Eddington Universalist Church.

During the Civil War years, no regular services were held. The parsonage that had been purchased in 1854 had to be sold due to lack of financial resources. During the period of 1873 to 1882, only transient preachers served the spiritual needs of the church parishioners.

In the summer of 1888, there was a desire among the parishioners to conform to the Universalist Creed and to form an association with both the Maine Universalists and the Universalist General Convention. On August 31, 1888, a set of bylaws were formulated for reorganizing the church to conform to the usages and requirements of the Universalists. A week later, at the next meeting, fifty-seven names were added to the membership of the new Universalist Parish of East Eddington.

One of the first items the newly reorganized church needed to deal with was what to do about the church building that had been badly neglected for nearly twenty years. Initial consensus was that money should be solicited to refurbish the old church. During the summer of 1889, discussions turned to the idea of building a new church.

On January 28, 1890, parish members voted to build a new church. A decision on the location of the new building was tabled for consideration at a later meeting, at which time a decision was reached to build the new church on the site of the original building. While construction of the new building was taking place, worship services were held in the public hall.

Work commenced on the new church building on August 13, 1890. A dedication service marked the laying of the cornerstone on September 6, 1890. The service was led by the Reverend H.F. Moulton, and he was assisted by the Reverend Charles Fisher of Canton, New York. Construction of the new church continued into the summer of 1891. On Sunday, September 5, 1891, the parishioners of the Universalist Parish of East Eddington held their first service in their new house of worship.

The fervor and activity of the church waned at the turn of the century. There were still people willing to work at keeping the church going, but few were Universalists. The church saw some additional new members during the years of World War I, but by 1924 the church was closed for an entire year. From 1925 to 1930, the church was reopened for the summer months. During the years of 1931 and 1932, there were no regular church services.

On May 18, 1937, a meeting was held at the public hall, also known as Comins Hall; those present wished to keep the church alive but were unwilling to sign the Universalist bylaws. Thus the beginning of what would become the East Eddington Community Church was initiated. It was not until December 17, 1951, that the parish was formally reorganized and incorporated as the East Eddington Community Church.

In 1990, the East Eddington Community Church celebrated its centennial anniversary and remains a special spiritual beacon for the region.

East Eddington Community Church was established circa 1890.

The East Eddington Community Church is located on Route 9 (the Air Line) in East Eddington. For additional information, telephone the pastor at (207) 944-5283.

## CLIFTON

### *Clifton United Baptist Church*

For nearly two centuries, the Clifton United Baptist Church has served as the spiritual center of this rural region that lies eighteen miles west of Bangor on Route 9 (the Air Line). On the cold, bleak day of November

19, 1838, a small band of hearty souls gathered to organize the Free Baptist Church of Jarvis Gore, which later was to be incorporated as the town of Clifton.

Charter members of the church were Eliphalet Bracket, Samuel DeBeck, William DeBeck, Leonard D. DeBeck, Hephzebeth DeBeck, Simon Crosby, Caleb Philbrick, Jarvis Penny, Orilla Rooks and Charity Staples.

In 1851, the name of the church was changed to the Clifton Free Baptist Church to reflect the town's incorporation. Construction of the church was started in 1855. The lovely white-framed church building that serves today as both a spiritual and physical landmark for the region was completed on September 13, 1889. On September 14, 1889, the congregation joined in offering the house to God. The dedication prayer was offered by the Reverend Howard A. Welch of Brewer; the congregation participated in the hymn, "Faith of Our Fathers," and benediction was given by the Reverend Louise Edwards of Brewer.

After the church affiliated with the American Baptist Convention, the name of the church was changed to the Clifton United Baptist Church.

To commemorate the church's ninetieth anniversary, a number of general renovations to the old church were made, both inside and out, including the installation of new pews and a bell. On July 1, 1928, a large group attended a rededication service with the Reverend A.M. Winsor of Bangor presiding.

In 1963, a Christian education addition was completed. This was the first major physical change to the church since its completion in 1889. A Founder's Day Celebration was held on Sunday, November 19, 1978, to celebrate the Clifton United Baptist Church's 140th anniversary. Special guests for this special day included former ministers of the church and representatives of the Maine State Baptist Conference. The pastor, the Reverend H.V. Nash, officiated at the celebration service.

Since 1992, the church has provided a vacation Bible school during the summer months for youth of the area. Many years this highly successful program has been jointly sponsored by the East Eddington Community Church. The summer months have also seen monthly "singspirations." Donations raised from these events have been used to purchase choir music and robes, as well as for equipment for the fellowship hall.

Many local Christians call the Clifton United Baptist Church their spiritual home.

Since September 2008, the worship service is opened by the Worship Team, which consists of teenagers and young adults. Today approximately twenty families are active members of the church.

The Clifton United Baptist Church is located at 742 Airline Road (Route 9). For more information, contact the Reverend John Walsh by telephone at (207) 843-5441.

*Chapter 2*

# Acadia's Religious Heritage

## Stonington

### *St. Mary Star of the Sea*

History of the area establishes the fact that Native Americans were there over six thousand years ago. Their descendents were known to early French explorers as Etchemins; some of these people continued to live on the island even after Anglo Americans established their settlements.

The town of Stonington was originally known as Green's Landing and was described as just a small remote fishing village on the larger island of Deer Isle. On February 18, 1897, the Maine legislature officially incorporated the town of Stonington. It was during this period of the late nineteenth century that this remote fishing village underwent an economic boom as a result of the development of granite quarrying. To work in this burgeoning industry, many Europeans, most from Italy, were imported to work as stone cutters.

It is not known for certain when a Catholic priest first celebrated Mass in Stonington. One native's recollection is that the first Mass was held in 1916 in the home of Frank and Annie McGuire. This may be related to the fact that the quarry industry on Hurricane Island had ended, and as a result, the Catholic Church there had been closed.

It is known that, in 1924, Annie McGuire started catechism classes in her home for young children in the area. Fifteen young Catholics in 1926 were taken by their parents to St. Joseph's Church in Ellsworth to receive the sacrament of Confirmation from the Portland Roman Catholic Diocese bishop, John Murray.

During that portion of the 1920s, priests from St. Joseph's Church in Ellsworth made occasional visits to Stonington to celebrate Mass and administer sacraments. Baptismal and marriage records of Stonington Catholics of that era can also be found at St. Joseph's. At some point during the late 1920s, pastoral responsibility for Stonington-area Catholics was transferred to the pastor of St. Ignatius's Church in Northeast Harbor.

In 1930, the Reverend John J. Beecher, pastor of St. Ignatius's Church, decided with the support of Catholics in the Deer Isle region to build a church in Stonington. Mr. Frank McGuire, as treasurer and chairman of the building committee, began to solicit donations and to purchase small lots that became the church property. The church building project team included architect, Frederick Patterson of Bangor; contractor, Basil Bray; foundation and grading, Calvin Ames; foundation and cellar, Arthur Poitras; cross and ball, Frank Judkins; and painting, B.C. Gardiner. The total cost of the project, exclusive of foundation work and painting, was $5,470. Major church furnishings included the gift by Isidor Gordon of a church bell cast in 1853 by Henry N. Hooper and Company of Boston. A holy water font of Vermont marble was contributed by Mr. and Mrs. F.R. Patch of Rutland, Vermont. The wooden altar rail was transported by the boat *Circe* from the abandoned church on Hurricane Island. Oak pews, a Gothic altar and Stations of the Cross were purchased for the new church at a total cost of $1,625.

On July 3, 1931, the first Mass was celebrated in the new church. Bishop John Murray formally dedicated the new church on October 4, 1931. In addition to the dedication ritual, the celebration of Mass and the confirmation of eleven children and two adults, Bishop Murray conducted Stations of the Cross and benediction of the Most Blessed Sacrament. The new church was filled to capacity on this joyous occasion by people of all faiths and creeds. The bishop concluded this auspicious day with the community by shaking hands with all in attendance.

The Reverend John Beecher remained pastor of the new mission church, St. Mary Star of the Sea, until September 9, 1934, when it received its first resident pastor, the Reverend Neil A. Burke. The parish records at St. Ignatius's, Northeast Harbor, show the baptisms and marriages performed at St. Mary Star of the Sea from the time the church was built until it ceased being a mission parish. Gilbert Charles Poitras was the first infant to be baptized in the new church on December 6, 1931. The first marriage was between Eric Bruno Thorbjornson and Adrea Bartlett, which was on August 19, 1931.

The first resident pastor on his arrival found that there were twenty-four Catholic families, with ninety-six members on Deer Isle and Little Deer Isle. During the four years that Reverend Burke served at St. Mary

St. Mary Star of the Sea Church in Stonington was completely refurbished in 1980.

Star of the Sea, he was responsible for the purchase of the parish rectory on Thurlow Hill and the purchase of land for a cemetery.

Between 1938 and 1980, eleven resident pastors served the spiritual needs of the parishioners of St. Mary Star of the Sea. In 1980, the church was completely refurbished. A Mass honoring the successful completion of this major undertaking was celebrated by the Reverend Eugene Gaffey on All Saints' Day 1980. On June 28, 1981, St. Mary Star of the Sea celebrated its fiftieth anniversary.

Today the church has approximately 150 year-round members from Deer Isle, Little Deer Isle, Sedgwick, Brooklin and parts of Brookville. Like most coastal communities, the summer season adds additional worshipers at St. Mary Star of the Sea.

St. Mary Star of the Sea is part of Cluster 11 and Deanery IV—Southern Penobscot, Hancock and Waldo Counties—and, as of 2008, is part of the Stella Maris Parish, together with Our Lady of Holy Hope, Castine and St. Vincent de Paul, Bucksport.

St. Mary Star of the Sea is located at 8 Granite Street. For additional information, contact the Stella Maris Office at 60 Franklin Street, Bucksport, Maine, 04416, by telephone at (207) 469-3322 or via e-mail at stellamaris@roadrunner.com.

## CASTINE

### *Unitarian Universalist Congregation of Castine*

In colonial days and in the years following the Revolution, the Congregational Church was the official church of Massachusetts. In order for a community to be incorporated as a town by the Commonwealth of Massachusetts, of which Maine was then a part, it was required that the community have a meetinghouse, which equated to a Congregational church.

The Unitarian Universalist Meeting House of Castine was built in 1790 and was originally called the First Congregational Society Meeting House. It served as a meetinghouse for religious services, as well as a facility for town meetings and special court sessions. The meetinghouse is steeped in history and posseses a steeple designed by Charles Bulfinch and a Revere bell. In 1820, it became the First Congregational Society, Unitarian.

A religious dispute arose after the Revolutionary War. The liberal Congregationalists, based at Harvard College, believed in human potential for self-improvement and believed that Jesus was human and God was one—a unity. Thus this group of believers came to be known as Unitarians. The conservative branch of the Congregationalists was based at Yale College. They believed in the depravity of humans and in the doctrine of the trinity. They were regarded as orthodox or Trinitarians. This conservative branch eventually became the Congregational denomination.

During the height of this religious controversy, the Reverend William Mason arrived to serve as Castine's first minister. A Harvard graduate, he held the liberal Unitarian view. He served from 1798 to 1834. In 1820, dissatisfied members of the congregation withdrew to form the Castine Trinitarian Church, which joined the new Congregational denomination. Following the split in the church and the removal of the county seat from Castine, the meetinghouse was remodeled in 1831 to accommodate a smaller congregation. After the retirement of the Reverend Mason, a short succession of Unitarian ministers served the Castine congregation.

Unitarian Universalist Congregation of Castine was built in 1790.

During the period from 1839 to 1850, the church

was served by Universalist ministers who were generally self-taught and from working-class backgrounds, in contrast to the Harvard educated Unitarians. After 1850, no minister served the church until the Unitarians revived the congregation in 1867.

Until 1990, the church was officially called the First Congregational Society Unitarian. In 2006, the church was renamed the Unitarian Universalist Congregation of Castine.

The congregation is a diverse community of individuals dedicated to promoting reason and freedom of religion, spiritual growth, ethical living and a better world. All are welcome to come and join on their spiritual journey. The Meeting House is located on Court Street on the Common.

For more information, call (207) 326-9083 or e-mail uucastine@verizon.net.

## *Our Lady of Holy Hope Chapel*

Castine, Maine, is one of North America's oldest communities, having been occupied continuously since the early 1600s as the site of trading posts, forts, missions and permanent settlements by France, Holland and England, as well as colonial America. For thousands of years, prior to Europeans discovering the Castine area, it had been the home to several Native American nations.

The site of an ancient Etchemin camping place stands directly in the location of the present-day Our Lady of Holy Hope Chapel. It is most probably the site of Betsabe's permanent camp of eighty wigwams and three hundred Native Americans. In November 1611, this site was visited by French explorer Biencourt and a Jesuit missionary, Father Biard, who celebrated Mass and ministered to the Native Americans in the area they named Pentagoet.

A year later, the peninsula region we know as Castine appears on a chart that explorer and geographer Samuel de Champlain submitted to King Henry IV of France. French records describe the location they called Pentagoet as being on the eastern side of what is now called Penobscot Bay. In 1613, the French established a trading post in the region that is believed to have been the first permanent settlement in New England.

In 1614, Captain John Smith charted the area and claimed it for England. Settlers named the area Majabagaduce. The signing of the Breda Treaty in 1667 ended the war between France and England, with Castine and the surrounding region being ceded to the French. A French officer, Jean Vincent d'Abbadie de St. Castin, received a grant from the king for land on the Pentagoet peninsula region. The community's name, Castine, dates back to this French officer.

Our Lady of Holy Hope Chapel stands on the site of Fort Pentagoet and was remodeled from an ancient structure. A historic copper plate was found at the site of the chapel that bore the English translation inscription "11 June 1648 Father Leo Capuchin, Paris."

On August 28, 1921, Our Lady of Holy Hope Chapel was dedicated on this historic site by Bishop Louis F. Walsh of the Portland Diocese. He was assisted by priests from Penobscot valley towns and Quebec, while Indians in native costumes added a picturesque touch to the ceremony. The Reverend Thomas J. Campbell, S.J. of New York gave the sermon for the dedication.

Our Lady of Holy Hope Chapel in Castine is on the site where a French missionary, Father Biard, ministered to an estimated three hundred Native Americans in November 1611.

Today Our Lady of Holy Hope is part of Cluster 11 and Deanery IV—Southern Penobscot, Hancock and Waldo Counties—and, as of 2008, is part of Stella Maris Parish, together with St. Mary Star of the Sea, Stonington and St. Vincent de Paul, Bucksport.

Our Lady of Holy Hope Chapel is located on Perkins Street. For additional information, contact the Stella Maris Office, located at 60 Franklin Street, Bucksport, Maine, 04416, by telephone at (207) 469-3322 or via e-mail at stellamaris@roadrunner.com.

## *Trinity Episcopal Church*

During the Revolutionary War the novice American naval force was annihilated by the British fleet in Castine Harbor in what became America's worst naval defeat up until Pearl Harbor. After the War of 1812, Castine flourished as a shipping port.

In the years following the Civil War, the sailing ships that plied the seas out of Castine went through a significant decline, and this resulted in the end of Castine's era of prosperity. During the late 1880s, Castine, like other Maine coastal communities, was rediscovered by summer vacationers from Boston, New York and Philadelphia who came by steamboats to escape the heat of the nation's large cities. During this period, Castine again flourished from the trade generated by these new folks, or "rusticators," as they were called by the locals. It was during this era that Trinity Chapel was built to provide for the spiritual needs of summering Episcopalians.

The 1,300-square-foot chapel was designed by Caroline Schenck and is an outstanding example of Arts and Craft architecture. In today's world, she would be seen as a green architect, as she desired that the chapel appear to grow naturally out of the landscape. Working with a small lot on sharply rising ground, she used only local building materials, including large amounts of Maine coast stone. In addition to her thoughtful environmental approach to the chapel's design, she used the landscaping to lead worshippers to the chapel steps for a dazzling view of the harbor. Schenck carried her dramatic design efforts to the interior space of the chapel to make it feel almost subterranean, with stone walls lit by small earth-tinted windows high on the side walls. Schenck intended for Trinity

Chapel to be a sanctuary for the worship of God and a special place for both prayer and meditation, where the soul may meet its creator, redeemer, sanctifier and blessed trinity.

In 1995, a parish hall was erected. It was designed to be architecturally compatible with the chapel, as well as triple the space for the growing needs of a year-round parish. The new addition allowed the parish to expand its visibility and outreach in the Castine community. Today it houses the only child care in the village of Castine. In 2006, the parish community called its first full-time rector, Reverend David Andrews. Father Andrews has been instrumental in spearheading social and outreach events in Castine and beyond. In both 2007 and 2008, Father Andrews, together with citizens from Castine, was part of two mission teams from the Episcopal Diocese of Maine to travel to New Orleans to spend a week assisting residents of that city find housing after the wake of Hurricane Katrina. Monies have been raised to help with Habitat for Humanity projects in that battered area, as well as to provide fuel assistance in the local area. The church has also expanded its outreach to the Castine-based Maine Maritime Academy.

Trinity Episcopal Church serves as a growing place for worship in the historic Castine community.

Trinity Episcopal Church is located at Perkins and Tarrantine Streets. For additional information, contact the pastor by telephone at (207) 326-4180 or by mail at P.O. Box 433, Castine, ME 04421.

## Blue Hill

### *First Congregational Church of Blue Hill, United Church of Christ*

On October 7, 1772, some ten years after the founding of the town of Blue Hill, eight men and six women of the community gathered to organize the First Congregational Church of Blue Hill. This was the first Congregational Church to be established east of the Kennebec River. The Reverend Daniel Little of Wells preached the first sermon, and the confession of faith ended with the prayer, "Now may the gracious and glorious covenant-keeping God forgive us all our offences, assist us and bless us in this covenant, and keep us now and forever in Jesus Christ, Our Lord. Amen"

A site in the Tide Mill district near Blue Hill Falls was chosen for their meetinghouse. The exact location remains unknown, although town records indicate that meetings took place there over a period of years. As the community grew, the need for a larger more centrally located meetinghouse was required. During this period, Maine was a part of the commonwealth of Massachusetts, and the Congregational Church was the commonwealth's official church. Meetinghouses at that time functioned as both a house for religious services and for civic activities of the community.

In May 1792, the framing and raising of the second meetinghouse in Blue Hill was initiated with a day of entertainment to commemorate the occasion. Town records show that the townspeople had voted for a barrel of rum, molasses and sugar for this event. The new fifty- by forty-foot meetinghouse building was modeled after the Old South Church in Boston and was located on the north side of Main Street near the top of Tenney Hill.

The first settled minister, the Reverend Jonathan Fisher, was called to serve in Blue Hill in 1796. This minister became in 1815 one of the founders of the Bangor Theological Seminary. He was known to have walked the thirty-six miles to Bangor to attend meetings of the newly formed seminary. In 1831, the Reverend Fisher published his first antislavery statement.

John Peters presented the town of Blue Hill with a Paul Revere bell for installation in the meetinghouse in 1821. On January 2, 1842, the meetinghouse burned to the ground.

The separation of church and state occurred in early 1842 as the result of a Blue Hill resident refusing to pay the compulsory church tax. He was jailed in Ellsworth for a month while the legal controversy was resolved. Since that time, all church funds have been raised by voluntary contributions.

The present church building was dedicated in January 1843. The perfectly proportioned Greek Revival architectural plans are credited to

The historic First Congregational Church of Blue Hill, Maine, UCC.

B.J. Deane, a Bangor architect, while members of the parish contributed the labor and materials. The bell now in the church is a recasting of the Paul Revere bell, which fell and broke during the old meetinghouse's fire.

In 1890, the interior walls of the meetinghouse were found to be in poor condition and were totally renovated to include stencil decorations in a High Victorian manner. Since then, the sanctuary has been redecorated several times, and six beautiful stained glass windows now adorn this historic meetinghouse.

The First Congregational Church of Blue Hill, United Church of Christ, strives to be an open and affirming congregation that freely offers full participation in services and sacraments and ordination for those who are qualified, affirm the church's covenant and desire to be part of the congregation. The church is located at 22 Tenney Hill.

For more information, call (207) 374-2891 or the pastor's study at (207) 374-2892.

## *St. Francis by the Sea Episcopal Church*

On June 15, 1975, eight Episcopalians met in the Blue Hill Library loft for a celebration of the Eucharist, with the Reverend Kenneth H. Anthony as the celebrant. Shortly thereafter, St. Francis by the Sea was recognized by the Diocese of Maine as a preaching station, with Father Anthony as first priest in charge.

During the next fifteen years, St. Francis by the Sea held its services in a variety of venues, including the Bar Harbor Bank and Trust, Rowantrees Pottery and, finally, at the American Legion Hall. In 1983, St. Francis became a mission of the diocese and installed its first vicar, the Reverend Richard Fenn. As part of the diocese's Down East Cluster, it shared vicars with churches in Bucksport, Castine and Stonington. In 1989, the congregation had grown to a point that it required more space for services, and in December, they purchased the old North Penobscot Methodist Church. The Reverend John Hedger became the congregation's first part-time priest in January 1990.

A year later, the old church building was physically moved to the church's present location on a parcel of land donated by Dr. and Mrs. Edward M. Leach. On Pentecost in 1991, St. Francis by the Sea celebrated its first Eucharist in its own home. Over the next fourteen months, significant renovations to the church were completed, and on May 2, 1992, the refurbished building was consecrated.

The Reverend Allan Sandlin became St. Francis by the Sea's first full-time vicar on Ash Wednesday 1994. During the next several years, regular attendance grew to about one hundred parishioners, and a number of programs were expanded, including a decision to dedicate one-half of the congregation's annual fair revenue to organizations serving others in the community. On May 17, 1996, St. Francis became a parish, with Father Sandlin as rector.

On March 19, 2000, major construction commenced on the church, and during this period, the parish moved its services in with their very generous friends at the First Congregational Church of Blue Hill, UUC, on Main Street. On February 25, 2001, with the major renovation project completed, the congregation returned to their home. St. Francis by the Sea's church building design is of a New England Colonial style. It provides a large undercroft for offices, social events, outreach, educational activities and a Sunday school/nursery. The nave can accommodate two hundred worshipers and houses a twenty-two-rank pipe organ, as well as a quarter-grand piano. The building's design allows for flexible use by parishioners and community groups.

During the years 2000 to 2003, there was serious dissension within the parish from both emotional and financial reverses, as well as from unexpected changing of rectors. By August 1, 2007, when the Reverend Claudia Smith became the third full-time rector of St. Francis by the Sea, the parish family was well on the road to its recovery.

The mission of St. Francis by the Sea is to glorify God and serve as a vital growing place for worship and education. The parish is known for its inclusiveness and an open Eucharist and welcomes all to be part of their congregation. Like most coastal Maine communities, summer brings many vacationers and folks with summer homes in the area, nearly doubling attendance at services.

St. Francis by the Sea Episcopal Church is located at 330 Hinkley Ridge Road, Blue Hill. For additional information, call (207) 374-5200.

St. Francis by the Sea Episcopal Church of Blue Hill was consecrated on May 2, 1992.

## Surry

### *Morgan Bay Zendo*

In 1971, Walter Nowick established the Moonspring Hermitage in Surry, Maine. When he stopped teaching at the center in 1985, the activities were renamed and reincorporated as the nonprofit Morgan Bay Zendo, offering an opportunity for people of any background or faith to practice Buddhist meditation.

Buddhist meditation is a means of developing the mind so that it may be awakened to its own inherent wisdom and compassion. At the Morgan Bay Zendo, one will find practices from the Zen, Ch'an and Vipassana schools of Buddhism.

Originally from India, Buddhism is based on four truths: all life is suffering; desire is the cause of suffering; there is a path one can follow out from suffering; and nirvana is the end of suffering. In most schools of Buddhism, meditation is the key to one's spiritual progress. While most people are constantly thinking of either the past or the future, in Zen you are trying to live in the present.

Nestled in a pristine setting in the coastal town of Surry is the zendo, a building designed in an authentic Japanese style as the complex's meditation hall. Other buildings in this rural campus setting include a meeting hall, four small cabins and a field for tent camping during the summer months. A pond, moss garden and wooded paths provide a perfect environment for meditation and retreats.

Sunday morning meditation is held at the zendo year-round from 9:00 to 11:00 a.m. Participants sit for twenty-five minutes, take a five minute break and then sit again for twenty-five minutes. A twenty-minute period of walking in the zendo is the next practice. Participants sit again, ending with a reading and Buddhist chanting. During the summer months there is Wednesday evening meditation from 7:00 to 8:00 p.m. Beginners without prior meditation are always welcome. Information and instruction is available, and introductory days are provided from time to time.

Retreats are scheduled throughout the year and are open to everyone. Vegetarian meals are served, and a modest fee is charged. The zendo is closed to visitors during retreats except for Sunday morning meditation.

Retreats and workshops explore a wide array of subjects, from applying age-old Zen Buddhist philosophy and living life in the twenty-first century to creating true peace even in the midst of conflict and showing the relationship of Zen to Celtic spirituality.

The Morgan Bay Zendo is located at 532 Morgan Bay Road. For more information, e-mail info@morganbayzendo.org or visit the website at www.morganbayzendo.org.

## Ellsworth

### *First Congregational Church, UCC*

The Ellsworth area was disputed between the English and the French throughout the seventeenth century and well into the eighteenth as a result of intermittent warfare known as the French and Indian War. After the signing of the Treaty of Paris in 1763 by the governments of England, France, Spain and Portugal, Ellsworth became part of Massachusetts. At that time, Ellsworth was known as Union River. Benjamin Milliken and Benjamin Joy were two of the area's earliest known settlers. Religious faith flourished during the late seventeenth century even though the Reverend Peter Nourse did not arrive as the community's first settled pastor until 1803.

In 1812, the Reverend Nourse organized the church and served in the dual role of pastor and village schoolmaster for twenty-three years. During his pastorate, the first meetinghouse was built on the present site in 1818 on land donated by Colonel Melatiah Jordon, who in addition bore the total expense of the building project. The new church was a large, white structure with a bell tower but no spire. It faced State Street, as Church Street did not exist at the time.

The Reverend Dr. Sewall Tenny was the Reverend Nourse's successor as pastor in 1835. The Reverend Dr. Tenny became a beloved minister, serving as pastor of the church for forty years. During his pastorate, a new church was constructed to accommodate the growing congregation. The building project commenced in 1847 under Thomas Lord, who during his professional career built fourteen churches in Hancock County. The beautiful First Congregational Church of Ellsworth is reputed to be one of the most photographed churches in New England. The church received its first pipe organ in 1854 from Colonel John Black. When the sanctuary was completely renovated in 1912, the grandson of Colonel John Black, George Nixon Black, gifted the church with a new organ.

Through the years, major renovations have been made to the church. In 1960, the present Christian education wing was built. In 1968, ambitious restorations and renewal plans were implemented, which included rebuilding of the pipe organ, completing the Sargent Memorial Chapel and installing the Thorsen Memorial Carillon. The church steeple was completely rebuilt in 1971. The 1990s saw renovation of the administration wing and the Sargent Memorial Chapel.

On April 24, 1973, the First Congregational Church of Ellsworth, with its illustrious history and wonderful example of early Greek Revival architecture, was duly recognized and entered into the National Register of Historic Places. On July 23, 1972, the church voted to become a participating member of the United Church of Christ.

For nearly two centuries, the church has provided spiritual joy and nourishment to its congregation, as well as service to the total community. The First Congregational Church, UCC, is located at 2 Church Street. For additional information, call (207) 667-8301.

The First Congregational Church, UCC, in Ellsworth was placed on the National Register of Historic Places in April 1973.

### *Unitarian Universalist Church of Ellsworth*

In 1835, religious liberals of the Ellsworth area organized to form a Unitarian Society. In 1837, they ordained the Reverend William D. Wisall as their first minister. He was a native of Milford, Massachusetts, and received his bachelor of arts degree from Harvard University in 1816 and graduated from Harvard's Divinity School in 1821. Before coming to Ellsworth, he had preached occasionally in Castine. In 1839, the Reverend Wissal was dismissed, and the congregation abandoned their efforts to maintain a Unitarian presence in Ellsworth at that time.

The First Unitarian Church was reestablished in 1865 under the ministry of the Reverend William Henry Savary. This Yale-educated minister was a man of tremendous zeal and enthusiasm. During his tenure, the First Unitarian Church of Ellsworth was built at the corner of Oak and Main Streets (at the site of the present S.K. Whiting Park). The new church was dedicated in 1867. Among his ministerial accomplishments in Ellsworth was his founding of the Unitarian Reading Club, a reading, discussion, music and poetry circle. During his seven-year ministry, he also served as the county supervisor of schools, where he was influential in changing the archaic system of primary and secondary education.

The Reverend William H. Lyon succeeded the Reverend Savary in October 1873. During his ministry, major renovations of the church building took place, including the raising of the foundation one story and the installing of a vestry. The popular minister transferred his pastorate to the First Unitarian Church of Brookline, Massachusetts, in June 1878.

The Reverend Silas Wright Sutton served as pastor from December 1902 to December 1907. He was a graduate of both Tufts College and Tufts Divinity School and came to Ellsworth after serving pastorates in Wisconsin, Connecticut, New York and Massachusetts. During his pastorate, his wife made possible a much needed redecoration of the church. Following his tenure as minister, he retired from active ministry, and the First Unitarian Church of Ellsworth closed for five years.

In November 1912, the Reverend Sydney Scott Booth came from Waterville, Maine, as pastor at large for Hancock County. During his two years of ministry in Ellsworth, he was instrumental in not only reopening the church for worship services but also in making major repairs and improvements to the building. The former residence of A.M. Hopkins on Pine Street was purchased by the Unitarian Society to serve as a parsonage. The Reverend John Wesley Tickle, who served as minister from 1914 to 1919, was the first pastor to reside in the parsonage.

Like the Unitarians, the Universalist Church roots stem from their New England founding in Gloucester, Massachusetts, during the late eighteenth century. In 1961, the two churches merged to become the Unitarian Universalist Association. The Reverends Rhys Williams and Ralph Heverson, summer residents of the area, collaborated in 1963 to initiate the Summer Visiting Ministers Series.

In 1968, the Reverend Richard B. Gibbs was asked to come to Ellsworth to help shepherd the congregation during its transition from their old downtown church to their new modern church in a pristine setting outside of town. The new Unitarian Universalist Church of Ellsworth was dedicated in 1971, and the community room was added in 1982.

Unitarian Universalist Church of Ellsworth, Maine, was dedicated in 1867.

All are welcome into congregation membership without any doctrinal test. The church believes that life's beauty is too great to be squeezed into narrow creeds or doctrines.

The Unitarian Universalist Church of Ellsworth is located at 121 Bucksport Road. For additional information, call (207) 667-4393 or e-mail minister@uuellsworth.org.

## *St. Joseph Catholic Church*

A little less than one hundred years after the 1763 settlement of Union River (Ellsworth's original name) by a party of English entrepreneurs, led by Benjamin Milliken and Benjamin Joy, the community saw a large influx of Irish as a result of the potato famine in Ireland, which forced them to immigrate. Many came over on the open wooden boats that carried Canadian lumber to England and Ireland and provided cheap return transit on the empty boats. A large number of the Irish who arrived in St. John, New Brunswick, wanted to go on to Boston, where they had relatives who would help them find work. Ellsworth became an important stopover for many of these Irish immigrants during the mid-nineteenth century. Some decided to stay and find a new life in Ellsworth. Their culture and religion were entirely different from the local Yankees. These differences created potential friction between the two groups. It was within this historical framework that Father John Bapst, a Swiss-born Jesuit, took up residence in Ellsworth in January 1853.

Father Bapst arrived in New York in July 1848 with a group of forty-four Swiss Jesuits who had been exiled from their homeland by a civil war. On August 7, 1848, Father Bapst took up his first assignment in Maine on the reservation of the Penobscot Nation on Indian Island. He, with a Father James Moore, S.J, was charged with restoring the Jesuits' mission in Maine. Father Bapst remained at Indian Island until September 2, 1851, when he moved to make his headquarters in Eastport. The Jesuits' Maine mission was to serve the spiritual needs of the growing Catholic population that was scattered throughout Maine and that was in danger of losing their faith due to lack of priestly care and parish life. At that time, the Jesuit mission circuit consisted of thirty-three stations. The sheer magnitude of the task and the geographic area that needed to be covered only allowed for each mission station to be visited for a few days six times each year. From Eastport there were stations on Louis Island, Calais, Robinston, Pembroke, Pleasant Point, Lubec, Trescott and Machias. Along or near the Penobscot River were stations at Cherryfield, Benedicta, Old Town, Frankfort, Bucksport, Belfast, Rockland, Thomaston and Ellsworth. On the Kennebec, there were Waterville and Skowhegan. To cover the towns and stations near Eastport was more than three priests could do, which made Bishop Fitzpatrick suggest developing another center nearer to the Penobscot. Ellsworth was considered to be the best location for this new center.

Catholics in the Ellsworth area had acquired a small building that was used as a chapel during the 1840s and early 1850s. As a mission station, it is most probable that the Reverend Thomas O'Sullivan, from the old St. Michael's Church in Bangor, was the first priest to hold services in Ellsworth on an occasional basis. Father Bapst made the construction of a new church a top priority for initiating the new central mission center. The new church was completed near the end of 1853.

During that period, it was the practice that parents bought the books that their children would use. Since everyone had a Bible, it had long been the custom to use it as a common reading book. The newly arrived Father Bapst became involved in an Ellsworth School Committee order that all students must read from the Protestant King James version of the Bible or be expelled from school. Father Bapst objected to this and requested in a petition to the Ellsworth School Committee that Catholic students be free to read from the Catholic Douay version of the Bible. The dispute could have been easily resolved if they followed the Bangor school officials' policy of allowing students to make their own personal choice in the matter. Since the school committee stuck to their order, Father Bapst, with the support of his parishioners, filed a suit against the town. This resulted in the fiery editor William H. Chaney of the *Ellsworth Herald* repeatedly attacking Father Bapst in his paper and warning the readers that their Irish servants would poison their food in order to wipe out Protestantism in the area. On June 3, 1854, a mob gathered at the rectory, and when told that Father Bapst was not in, they broke some windows. A few days later, the mob returned to attack the church, and thanks to the intervention by Colonel Charles Jarvis, only minor damage occurred. Fearing for Father

Bapst's life, Bishop Fitzpatrick transferred him to Bangor. The transfer did not suppress the anti-Catholic/anti-immigrant wave known as the Know-Nothing movement that was spreading in Ellsworth, as well as across the country. William H. Chaney, a vocal champion for the Know-Nothings, kept the controversy raging. On October 14, 1854, Father John Bapst went to stay the night at the home of the Richard Kent family in Ellsworth on his way to attend a sick call in Cherryfield. That evening a local Ellsworth gang called the Cast Iron Band found out that he was back in town, dragged him from the house, beat him, took his wallet and watch, stripped him, tarred and feathered him, tied him to a rough plank and carried him out to the woods where they left him. Thankfully he was found by friends who took him in, cleansed him and helped him get back to Bangor. In Bangor, he helped organize the building of St. John's Catholic Church on York Street. Father Bapst was transferred in 1858 to Boston, where he helped raise funds for the construction of Boston College. In August 1863, Father John Bapst was elected the new college's first president.

The original St. Joseph's Catholic Church in Ellsworth was completed in 1853.

St. Joseph's first Catholic Church in Ellsworth, which was built on the site of the present-day Mobil Station on Route 1, was deliberately burned to the ground, along with an unoccupied home of a parishioner, on April 27,

1857. Father Caraher became the first permanent pastor in Ellsworth and was responsible for the building of the second St. Joseph's Church in Ellsworth on Chapel Street during the 1860s. During the late 1880s, the parish increased in numbers and religious strength and saw major renovation projects completed, including the placement of a bell in the church tower.

The present St. Joseph's Church was completed in 1939. Today St. Joseph's Catholic Church, located at 231 Main Street, is a part of Deanery IV—Southern Penobscot, Hancock and Waldo Counties—and Cluster 11. During the summer months, St. Joseph's provides weekend Masses at George Stevens Academy in Blue Hill, Our Lady of the Lake in Green Lake, Dedham and St. Margaret Chapel in Winter Harbor, in addition to services at St. Joseph's Church in Ellsworth. For additional information, contact the parish office by telephone at (207) 667-2342 or via e-mail at stjosephoffice@choiceonemail.com.

## Bar Harbor

### *Maine Sea Coast Mission*

At the dawn of the twentieth century, two brothers, Alexander and Angus McDonald, who were both Congregational ministers, knew of the hardships faced by those living on Down East Maine's outer islands and were committed to making a difference in their lives. They approached their Christian challenge in an unorthodox manner for members of the clergy by attending first to the physical needs of these people. Rooted in compassion and justice, the two brothers founded the Maine Sea Coast Mission in 1905. To initiate their mission they purchased for $600 their first boat, the *Hope*. She was a twenty-six-foot wooden sailing sloop equipped with an auxiliary engine. In 1905, she plied the waters of the Gulf of Maine and helped to safely launch the voice of the mission.

It soon became apparent to the mission founders that a more capable boat than the *Hope* was needed to adequately do the work required. Help soon came from a member of their board, Bishop Alexander Mackay Smith of Philadelphia, who donated his personal boat, the *Virginia*, in

1906 to replace the *Hope*. It was renamed the *Morning Star* and remained in service until 1915.

The *Sunbeam* was the first of five boats to bear the name *Sunbeam* and to be specifically built for mission service. *Sunbeam I* was a fifty-seven-foot long vessel with a thirteen-foot beam. It was built of oak and yellow pine and was equipped with two gasoline-powered engines at a cost of $7,000. A Bar Harbor resident and longtime mission supporter, Mrs. John S. Kennedy, donated the funds for the boat. On April 6, 1912, it was launched with the words "I name thee *Sunbeam*, that thou might bring the gospel of sunshine and gladness to all parts of the coast." Expanding needs of the mission, as well as age factors, saw replacement of *Sunbeam* vessels through the years. The fifth vessel to proudly bear the name *Sunbeam* was launched at Boothbay in 1995.

As a nondenominational, nonprofit organization, the Maine Sea Coast Mission continues today to provide a source of hope, encouragement and strength to individuals, families and communities in Hancock and Washington Counties, as well as on the state's outer islands. Among the mission's programs are emergency financial assistance, Food Pantry

The *Sunbeam V*, belonging to the Main Sea Coast Mission in Bar Harbor, launched 1995.

and Thrift Shop, Sunbeam Island Health and Ministries to Island and Coastal Communities. In response to Washington County's high rate of school dropouts, substance abuse and youth suicide, the Maine Sea Coast mission developed EDGE, an innovative and comprehensive approach to education and youth development that is forging connections between in-school and out-of-school learning, student and teacher, child and family, as well as school and community.

Although much has changed in the culture and morals of our society since Alexander and Angus MacDonald founded the Maine Sea Coast Mission, their vision of providing help and comfort, as well as healing broken spirits, endures.

The Maine Sea Coast Mission is located at 127 West Street. For more information, call (207) 288-5097 or visit the website at www.seacoastmission.org.

### *Holy Redeemer Roman Catholic Church*

On March 21, 1613, Samuel de Champlain set sail from St. Croix Island, a small island in the St. Croix River that is just off shore from Calais, Maine, and separates the United States from New Brunswick, Canada, for a voyage of discovery along the coast. His ship, called the *Jonas*, was a one-hundred-ton vessel under the command of Captain Pierre la Saussaye. These French explorers eventually reached a large and beautiful island harbor that the Indians called Pemetic, which means a range of mountains seen from a distance. Champlain, the mapmaker and chronicler of the expedition, named the island discovery Isle de Monts Desert (island of deserted mountains). On board the *Jonas* were Jesuit missionaries led by Fathers Pierre Biard, Ennemond Masse and Jacques Quentin and Brother Gilbert du Thet. In May 1613, they went ashore to establish a mission to bring Christianity to the natives of Acadie, France's North American colony. Upon their landing, they raised a cross and celebrated Mass. The missionaries named their mission Saint Sauveur, or Holy Redeemer.

At this time, England and France were at war, and both countries laid claim to this same New World area. In September 1613, an English ship out of the Virginia colony under the command of Captain Argall destroyed the newly established mission, killed Brother du Thet and took the Jesuit priests prisoners. At a later date, the priests were returned to France. The Bar Harbor site of the Saint Sauveur Mission is known today as Jesuit Field and Jesuit Spring at the entrance to Somes Sound.

During the 1880s, many wealthy Americans from Boston, New York and Philadelphia discovered the pristine island of Mount Desert as a summer retreat and began flocking to the town of Eden (renamed Bar Harbor in 1918). During this time, there was no priest to attend to the spiritual needs of the growing number of Catholics. Occasionally a priest would come and celebrate Mass at a schoolhouse or at one of the fashionable hotels that had sprung up. A plan emerged in the summer of 1880 to build a church as the result of a donation of a parcel of land on Kebo Street by Mr. DeGrasse Fox and Mr. Brooks White. The plan for the church structure was designed by a well-known Boston architect, W.R. Emerson. It called for a forty- by seventy-foot wooden building capable of seating three hundred persons. Contributions for the planned church immediately started to materialize, and by the fall, sufficient funds had been collected to start the building project. The church was erected during the winter and spring months, and the first Mass was held in July 1881. The bishop placed the new church under the temporary charge of a visiting English priest, the Reverend J.R. Madan. The church was given the name of St. Sylvia and was then made a mission of St. Joseph's Church in Ellsworth. On August 13, 1882, St. Sylvia was officially dedicated by Bishop James Healy of the Diocese of Portland. This solemn event commemorated the return of the Catholic Church to Mount Desert and the fulfillment of the promise that the French Jesuits had made in the summer of 1613.

During the remainder of the nineteenth century, St. Sylvia flourished. The church added a large bell in 1884, and during the winter of 1886, when the church was closed, the seating capacity was increased to five hundred persons. Even with this increase and the addition of a vestry that served as a winter chapel, St. Sylvia was no longer adequate for its growing congregation.

In 1907, St. Sylvia became a parish with a full-time priest. The new pastor, the Reverend James D. O'Brien, decided that the time had come to build a new church, and on August 11, 1907, Bishop Walsh laid the cornerstone for the new church. It was to be made of stone with a slate roof and have a seating capacity of eight hundred to one thousand persons. The interior was constructed of open work finished in natural cypress. The new church was named Holy Redeemer in memory of the Jesuit Mission of Saint Sauveur that was established in July 1613. The name of St. Sylvia was given to the chapel that was constructed below the main church. The furnishings and holy articles of St. Sylvia's became a part of the new church. In 1911, the Church of St. Sylvia was razed, and the wood from the building was used to build a rectory below the new church on Ledgewood Avenue.

The year-round membership remained relatively small, while attendance during the summer blossomed. Many of the parishioners were domestic help of the wealthy cottage owners. There were some wealthy Catholic cottage owners, including General and Mrs. Edward Morrell of Philadelphia, who were generous benefactors to their summer parish. They donated the land and a house for a convent and provided the funds for the building of a parochial school. From 1913 to June 1967, St. Edwards School provided a Catholic educational opportunity for children on Mount Desert Island.

America's second native-born saint, Mother Katharine Mary Drexel, was the sister of summer resident Louise Drexel Morell, whom she visited regularly in Bar Harbor. The Drexel sisters were the daughters of Francis Anthony Drexel, a wealthy Philadelphia banker. Traveling in the western United States with their father, they encountered the hardship of American Indians and appealed to the American bishops to institute the annual national collection for black and Native Americans. Katharine entered the Sisters of Mercy in Pittsburgh and, in 1891, founded the Sisters of the Blessed Sacrament. Katharine and Louise directed the $14 million estate of their late father to be used by the new religious order's mission to the pastoral care and education of black and Native Americans. She was responsible for the founding of 145 missions, 12 schools for Native Americans and 50 schools, including Louisiana's Xavier University for African Americans. Saint Katharine died in 1955 and was canonized by Pope John Paul II on October 1, 2000.

For over a century Holy Redeemer Church has been serving the spiritual needs of both year-round parishioners and summer visitors.

Holy Redeemer Church is part of Deanery IV—Southern Penobscot, Hancock and Waldo Counties—and Cluster 11. Holy Redeemer provides weekend Mass for St. Ignatius Church in Northeast Harbor and St. Peter's in Manset and during the summer months at Our Lady of the Sea on Little Cranberry Island, Islesford. Holy Reedemer Church is located at 56 Mount Desert Street. Collectively, these churches comprise the Transfiguration Parish. For more information, contact the parish office by telephone at (207) 288-3535, e-mail at holyredeemer@roadrunner.com or by mail at 21 Ledgelawn Avenue, Bar Harbor, ME, 04609-1303.

## *St. Saviour's Episcopal Church*

St. Saviour commemorates the name that a group of French Jesuits led by Father Pierre Biard gave to a mission they established on Mount Desert Island in May 1613. The newly established mission was destroyed in September by an English vessel out of the Virginia colony under the command of Captain Argall. Three of the Jesuit priests were taken prisoner and Brother Gilbert du Thet was killed in the skirmish. When the war between France and England ended, the priests were returned to France.

The historical roots of St. Saviour's may be traced to 1863 when Jonathan Stevens built a schoolhouse in Hulls Cove, which was also to be used during the summer months as a mission church for both Hulls Cove and Bar Harbor. The period following the Civil War saw the rise of summer residents to the area. During the 1870s, services were also held at the Rodick House hotel in Bar Harbor. The growing summer residents decided to establish a church to nourish their spiritual needs, and in 1878, the first parish church was built. Bishop Henry A. Neely consecrated the new mission church on August 21, 1879. The bishop then appointed the Reverend Christopher Starr Leffingwell as its first vicar. The Reverend Leffingwell served the mission church for twenty years, plus three additional years as rector emeritus before his elevation to a canonry.

The parish's first governing body was known as the Committee for the Administration of Worldly Affairs of the Church, although it was commonly referred to as the vestry. It began its church operations in

1882, and its members were appointed by the bishop of Maine. Old meeting minutes show that membership included the names of many prominent men from Boston and New York. In later years, as the parish grew, the vestry was elected by parishioners, and the rector presided over their meetings.

During the years that Father Leffingwell served the fledging St. Saviour's mission church, he saw his congregation grow from a handful of communicants to 171, as well as the building of the mission Church of Our Father in Hulls Cove. Upon Father Leffingwell's retirement, his assistant, the Reverend William O. Baker, was appointed by Bishop Neely on June 26, 1899, as vicar.

Through the generosity of the new vicar's mother and father-in-law, Mr. and Mrs. Charles Carroll Jackson, St. Saviour's rectory was built in an architectural style of Bar Harbor homes of the late 1890s. In memory of Mr. Jackson's death, his widow built the Chapel of St. Mary and paid for the remodeling of the interior of the church to provide space for the boys' choir. In 1903, St. Saviour's status was changed from mission to parish, and a parish hall was built and dedicated to Father Leffingwell, who had died in 1902. The new parish hall provided an opportunity for greater activity among the various parish organizations. Through the years, the hall has served as an industrial school for training young people of the community in skills useful for employment in the Bar Harbor summer colony, as well as a meeting facility, a gymnasium and navy barracks during both world wars.

St. Saviour's is blessed with having ten of Louis Comfort Tiffany's beautiful stained glass windows, as well as a number of more formal English stained glass windows. These windows came to grace St. Saviour's as memorial gifts from 1886 to 1992. It is claimed that more Tiffany windows can be found at St. Saviour's than anywhere else in Maine.

A new world, in terms of lifestyle, emerged after World War I, which became known as the Jazz Age of the 1920s. This new age saw Prohibition become part of the law of the land, as well as women being given the right to vote. The October 1929 stock market crash wiped away the fortunes of many of the wealthy and notably diminished the once lavish lifestyle of the Bar Harbor summer colony. These hard times were followed by America's entrance into World War II as a result of the December 7, 1941 bombing of Pearl Harbor. In 1942, Father Russell Hubbard became St. Saviour's fourth rector. The U.S. Navy was once again barracked in the parish hall, and the church's ten-bell carillon played the "Navy Hymn" each noon; once the rector's wife startled the Bar Harbor community by varying this with "Coming in on a Wing and a Prayer." The Hubbards played a leadership role in both the community and diocesan affairs, as well as in relief work after the Great Fire of 1947 that decimated the region. The fire was the *coup de grace* for the summer colony, as many never returned after their cottages were destroyed. Of the 150 families that were burned out, 42 were communicants of St. Saviour's. Of even greater importance to the area was the loss of year-round employment.

The once fabulous Bar Harbor was a thing of the past during the late 1940s and early 1950s, but hope springs eternal and allows a community to begin to look ahead rather than behind. Liturgical renewal, outreach programs and ecumenical cooperation have all been hallmarks of the parish's ongoing vigor.

St. Saviour's identifies itself as an "open church," which means that all persons, wherever they are in their spiritual journey, are welcome to come and be a part of the church community. The communion meal of Christ's presence among us in the form of bread and wine is offered to anyone who comes with a sincere heart to receive it. Nursery care is available on Sunday. During July and August, there are free guided tours of the historic church, featuring its renowned collection of stained glass windows.

St. Saviour's Episcopal Church is located at 41 Mount Desert Street. For more information, call (207) 288-4215 or e-mail stsaviour@roadrunner.com.

### *Messenger of Peace: Father Jim Gower*

Jim Gower is a Bar Harbor native. His parents had come to the Acadia area to work where they met, married and settled. His father migrated there from Calais to ply his carpenter trade for the growing summer colony. His mother was an Irish lass who came to Bar Harbor to work as a maid in the homes of the wealthy. She was a Roman Catholic, and his father was a Baptist.

After graduating from high school, Jim applied and was accepted to both the University of Maine at Orono and the University of Notre Dame. There was a $10 difference in the tuition rate of the two schools: the University of Maine was $620 per academic year, whereas Notre Dame was $630. His mother encouraged him to matriculate at Notre Dame. He only had enough money to take him through one year, but his mother told him that the tuition money would turn up.

In the fall of 1941, Jim Gower, with his packed suitcase, hit the road for South Bend, Indiana. To conserve his meager financial resources, he thumbed his way to the school. In 1942, the Navy ROTC program arrived on the Notre Dame campus. Jim joined up, as this was a way for him to afford future tuition. In 1944, he graduated with a bachelor of science degree in naval science and went directly into naval service as an ensign. He served aboard ships in both the Atlantic and Pacific theaters during World War II and was discharged as a lieutenant. He returned briefly to Notre Dame to receive a second bachelor's degree in philosophy. He then entered the workforce with General Electric, and after six months in the corporate world, he decided that he would enter law school and possibly later pursue a political career. In the fall of 1947, he started Georgetown University Law School under the G.I. Bill and held a job in the Washington office of one of Maine's U.S. senators.

After a semester, Jim decided that he was not cut out for a career in the law. He also learned that politics required too much compromise, and one could not accomplish the goals of justice that he hoped for. This sparked his vocation for the priesthood.

In the fall of 1948, he entered Boston College for courses in theology, and after completing these studies, he went to St. Augustine Seminary in Toronto, Ontario. On May 30, 1953, he was ordained to the priesthood at the Cathedral of the Immaculate Conception in Portland, Maine, by Bishop Feeney.

After ordination, Father Jim Gower served in various parishes in the Portland Diocese and enjoyed being involved in his pastoral assignments. He was aware of the many injustices in the world but did not become actively involved until the Catholic chaplain from the University of Maine challenged him on what he was doing for the cause of peace and justice.

Father Jim said that the seeds for his becoming involved were probably planted early in life, starting during the Great Depression. He remembers his father saying shortly before Franklin Roosevelt was elected president that if something didn't happen soon, they would have to march on Washington. In the time following the market crash of 1929, those working in the trades, as well as many of the wealthy summer residents, found themselves in very serious financial straits. Unfortunately, in desperate times, many turn to desperate measures. During his World War II duty as a gunnery officer, he was fired on but never felt personally endangered, but he observed firsthand the devastation and sadness of war. During the Vietnam War, four young men from his Waterville Parish were killed in the line of duty. Meditating on the challenge he had been given in the context of violence going on in Southeast Asia, Father Jim decided that he needed to do something.

After spending a sabbatical in Rome discerning what the appropriate path was for him, he returned to the Portland Diocese and was assigned in 1972 as chaplain to the University of Maine at Orono. He soon heard of a Pax movement in England, which had a U.S. counterpart called Pax Christi, which was being directed by Eileen Egan, a woman who was closely associated with Mother Teresa. Father Jim was soon involved with Pax Christi. He didn't know exactly what he could do in the Acadia region of Maine, where he was serving, but soon found other like-minded people who wanted to start a college dedicated to peace and environmental issues. Their concept evolved into what was first called the Acadia Peace College but was finally named College of the Atlantic. Father Jim played a role in bringing the concept to fruition and is still active as a member of the college's board of trustees.

Recognizing that Pax Christi needed someone to go out and talk about the movement at churches, schools, retreat houses and seminaries, Father Jim asked Bishop O'Leary if he could take on this mission. For two years, Father Jim traversed the country, logging twenty-five thousand miles delivering a message of peace to all who would listen.

It was not until 1983 that the Catholic Church in America spoke out for peace at a U.S. bishops' conference in their paper, "The Challenge of Peace." A decade later, the bishops repeated their statement for peace.

Father Jim Gower, a messenger of peace, Bar Harbor.

The escalation of weapons of mass destruction by more and more nations and terrorist groups places the planet and all mankind in jeopardy. The violence will not stop until each individual stops being violent. The song "Let There Be Peace on Earth and Let It Begin with Me" says it all.

Although retired from the active priesthood and an octogenarian, Father Jim helps out in parishes throughout eastern Maine and plans to continue an active peace ministry.

*Chapter 3*

# A Faith of Our Fathers Tour Way Down East

## Winter Harbor

### *Channing Chapel*

The small sea coast village of Winter Harbor was originally known as Mosquito Harbor and was officially part of Township Number Three, Plantation of Gouldsboro, County of Lincoln in the commonwealth of Massachusetts. The early history of Winter Harbor is closely tied to that of Gouldsboro until it separated and became a separate town in 1895.

During the late 1800s and early 1900s, Winter Harbor was the scene of a bustling summer colony, with wooden walks along the beach, large cottages of wealthy families from Boston, New York and Philadelphia; hotels; restaurants; and shops. In 1887, David Flint, a wealthy summer resident from Boston, made a decision to build a Unitarian chapel on land adjacent to his large cottage. Flint was a lumber merchant who, after becoming wealthy, enjoyed sharing his prosperity as a philanthropist with many causes. He came to Winter Harbor in 1880 when Dr. Almena Guptill Baker, a Winter Harbor native who was practicing medicine in Boston and caring for his ailing wife, suggested that Mrs. Flint's health might improve by summering in Winter Harbor.

Being a staunch follower of William Ellery Channing, David Flint wished to provide a place for liberal Christian worship for both local families and summer residents. During the winter of 1887–88, beach and field stones were selected and brought to the site of the future chapel.

Construction of the chapel began in the spring of 1888, and on August 28, 1888, the chapel was officially dedicated to Dr. William Ellery Channing. About three hundred people, many from Boston, came for the all-day dedication ceremony. The local Beacon and Hanover Hotels provided the out-of-town guests' accommodations and dining. The chapel's stonework and magnificent stained glass windows were part of the architectural design of Arthur Rotch, of Rotch and Tilden of Massachusetts. The truss timbers and rafters of the chapel are of old oak, while cherry was used for the finished wood work. Two hundred people could be comfortably seated in the auditorium, with space for up to an additional seventy-five people in the vestry/library. Through the years, many notables of the day spoke at the chapel, including Booker T. Washington and Edward Everett Hale.

After the death of David Flint's first wife, he married Dr. Almena Guptill Baker, who was a widow. Their marriage provided David Flint

On August 29, 1888, the Channing Chapel in Winter Harbor was dedicated to the founder of Unitarianism.

with even stronger ties to Winter Harbor. In 1888, after completion of the chapel, David Flint had the property deeded to the Unitarian Society. It held ownership of the chapel until 1954 when the society gave it to the town of Winter Harbor. The town in turn sold the property for conversion to a private residence. The property went through several private ownerships, as well as serving as the town library.

In July 1993, as the result of generous donations, the building became owned by the Channing Chapel Preservation Society. Today the Channing Chapel serves as Winter Harbor's library. Channing Chapel is located on Chapel Lane.

For additional information, visit the website at www.winterharbor.lib.me.us.

## Milbridge

### *Milbridge United Methodist Church*

Four short years after the town of Milbridge was incorporated, the Union Society of Milbridge decided that the time was right for their community to have its own house of worship. A property was selected at the site of the present-day intersection of Wyman Road and Main Street to build their church. The church was completed in 1852 and was originally known as the Methodist Episcopal Church.

Prior to the building of the church, the spiritual needs of the local community were served by circuit riders, itinerant ministers who brought the gospel to folks scattered across eastern Maine.

The new church was partially financed and supported by a method called "pew ownership." An individual or a family paid for their own pew, which they used when they attended any church service. Evidence of these early pews can still be found in the church even years after their removal.

No historical record of either the circuit riders who preached or early ministers of the church were documented. The first minister to be clearly associated with the Milbridge Methodist Episcopal Church was the Reverend H.E. Frohock, who led a major repair and remodeling of the church in 1885. This project was funded by the sale of the parsonage together with donations from the parishioners. At about this same time, an arrangement was made with the pew owners to transfer their property right to the Methodist Society (Conference).

A federation was formed in 1925 between the Milbridge United Methodist Church and the Congregational Church of Milbridge, and worship services were alternated between the two churches until the federation was dissolved in 1973.

Through the years, normal repairs and maintenance were performed, and in 1926, electricity was installed in the church. No structural changes or major renovations projects were undertaken until 1993. At that time, a new foundation was installed and a new roof and steeple were added.

In 1852, the Union Society built the Milbridge United Methodist Church at the triangle of Wyman Road and Main Street. The church was originally known as the Methodist Episcopal Church.

The original steeple had been hit by lightning in 1939 and was in need of replacement.

Since its founding over a century and a half ago, the historic Milbridge United Methodist Church has not only served as a house of worship for its parishioners, but it has also reached out to provide counseling and service to the greater community during times of war and natural disasters and has as its mission to continue to help and serve the community.

The Milbridge United Methodist Church alternates its worship services with the Wyman United Methodist Church and both are spiritually served by the same pastor. The Milbridge United Methodist Church is located on Main Street (Route1), Milbridge, Maine.

### *Wyman United Methodist Church, Milbridge*

The town of Milbridge is a seacoast community located at the head of Narraguagus Bay in Washington County. It was incorporated by the legislature in 1848. A small village within the area was originally known as Pearl Districts 1 and 2 but with village unification became known as Wyman, in honor of the Wyman brothers who had played key local roles.

The Wyman brothers—Joseph D., John F., Jesse A., James T., Jasper, Frederick, Edgar, Chandler C. and Adelbert—had all been a part of the local village business community from their youth. Jasper successfully built a canning factory that employed many from the village. When the brothers learned that their friends and neighbors desired a house of worship, they proposed to build a church on the condition that members of the proposed church would contribute all furnishings and equipment. The fledging congregation accepted the Wyman brothers' offer, and the dream for a church was initiated. As the carpenters began construction of the church, parishioners were busy going door to door throughout the village, requesting donations to help make their dream a reality.

As of August 6, 1906, the newly completed Wyman United Methodist Church had been fully furnished and free of all debt when it celebrated its formal dedication. The Reverend T.J. Dienstadt, pastor of the new church, delivered the sermons at the two inaugural services, and Ms. Edith Flagg was organist for the dedication.

Prior to the building of the new church, services were held in a schoolhouse on Beal's Hill in Wyman village. Soon after the dedication of the new church, the women of the congregation established the Ladies Aid Society of Wyman for the purpose of providing ongoing support for activities such as church maintenance. To achieve their financial goals, they sponsored a variety of activities, including ice cream socials, suppers, concerts and quilting parties. Many men of the congregation were fishermen, and each of them designated the proceeds of one of their traps for the church. This project became known as the Lobster Trap Fund.

Among the new church benefactors were John Beal of Beals Island, who donated the church bell, and Obediah Ward of Cherryfield, who provided a communion service set. Other generous parishioners donated the chairs, pulpit and new Bible.

The Wyman United Methodist Church was built and dedicated in 1906.

Through the years, a number of renovations were made to the building. As the Wyman United Methodist Church prepared for its centennial anniversary, a number of significant renovations to the historic church were made, including new windows, vinyl siding and several roof repairs, while the interior had a complete makeover, with a new suspended ceiling, major electrical work, a new furnace and a total redecoration of all walls and woodwork.

On September 10, 2006, the Wyman United Methodist Church celebrated its 100th anniversary. The day's program opened with a historical slide show by Alison Woodward Wallace, with Alora and Debra Felix providing special music. Pastor Steve Smith and organist Greg Grant replicated some of the original 1906 dedication service.

The Wyman United Methodist Church, together with its sister church, the Milbridge United Methodist Church, provides for the spiritual well being of the community. Both churches are served by the same pastor, and services are alternated between them. The Wyman United Methodist Church is located on Wyman Road.

## Cherryfield

### *St. Michael's Catholic Church*

The historic village of Cherryfield was first settled in 1757 by Ichabod Willey, a New Hampshire native. After his arrival in this Way Down East community, he built a log cabin on what became known as Willey Hill. He then returned to New Hampshire to move his family to their new home. Additional settlers arrived during the late 1700s, including Alexander Campbell, the father of Cherryfield lumber industry, and General Campbell, who arrived and built his home on Campbell Hill in 1790. During the early nineteenth century, Cherryfield continued to see its population expand, which coincided with the arrival of Irish immigrants. While no historical records precisely document these early arrivals, there are some unsubstantiated data that indicate that some Irish Catholic immigrants could have been living in the area as early as the late 1820s.

By the summer of 1850, it is well documented that many thousands of Catholics were scattered over eastern Maine and were on the circuit stations covered by Father John Bapst, a Swiss Jesuit missionary. Cherryfield was one of ten circuit stations that Father Bapst served.

Ten years later, in 1864, a determined group of Catholics banded together to build St. Michael's Church in Cherryfield. These first parishioners paid $5,000 for the small parcel of land that became the site of their church. This dollar amount was excessive at the time for the very small piece of land involved and indicated that the local non-Catholics were not too happy with a growing Catholic population in their community. Thankfully, the money was raised to make St. Michael's become a reality.

On January 22, 1874, James Mahaney and Peter Smith conveyed by Warranty Deed Number 503 the property transfer for $3,500 to Bishop David Bacon. The first Catholic priest to officiate at the new mission church of St. Joseph's in Ellsworth was Father Madden. Traveling by horse and buggy, Catholics from Addison, Beddington, Cherryfield, Centerfield, Columbia, Columbia Falls, Deblois, Milbridge and Steuben came to attend Mass. The church was lit by gasoline lanterns and heated by a wood stove.

A steeple can be seen in old photos of St. Michael's circa 1864–65. According to an account by Charlie Wakefield, who died many years ago, the steeple was found piercing the lawn in front of the church after a bad storm. No one seems to know what happened to the steeple after that.

In the 1930s and '40s, St. Michael's remained a mission of St. Joseph's in Ellsworth. The pastor of St. Joseph's would take the early train from Ellsworth and return on the late train. There were no Masses during the winter.

It was not until the Reverend Lionel J. Chouninard became pastor of Holy Name Church in Machias and St. Michael's was a mission of Holy Name in Machias that there were Masses celebrated year-round in Cherryfield. Winter Masses initially were held at the Weald Bethel Chapel in Cherryfield and then at the Cherryfield Town Office.

In 1986, a fundraiser was organized for the purpose of building a new foundation for the church. On April 11, 1896, John P. Harriman

St. Michael's Catholic Church, Cherryfield, was built in 1864 to serve as a summer seasonal parish.

generously sold to St. Michael's, for consideration of one dollar, a quarter of an acre of land to build the new foundation to house the church, as well as provided parking space for parishioners. St. Michael's had a new beginning in 1990 when the building was moved to its new foundation. The new heated church basement provided adequate space for celebrating Mass during the winter months.

During the late twentieth century and through the current era, St. Michael's has continued to grow with an active and diverse congregation. St. Michael's Church is in Deanery III (Washington County) and Cluster 10, as well as being part of the recently structured St. Peter the Fisherman Parish, together with Holy Name Church in Machias, Sacred Heart in Lubec and St. Timothy's in Campobello Island, New Brunswick. St. Michael's Church is located on Elm Street. For additional information, contact the parish office by writing 11 Free Street, P.O. Box 248, Machias, ME, 04654-0248, call (207) 255-3731 or e-mail at stpeterthefisherman@portlanddiocese.org.

## JONESPORT

### *Sawyer Memorial Congregational Church*

Jonesport is a small seacoast town on a peninsula at Chandler Bay and beside Englishman Bay in Washington County. It was settled in the years preceding the Revolutionary War and was originally a part of Jonesboro under a grant given to a John Jones and other settlers by the Massachusetts General Court. On February 3, 1832, it was separated from Jonesboro and incorporated as Jones' Port.

In the late 1790s and into the 1880s, many Jonesport church-going residents were members of the Machias Centre Street Congregational Church, whose history dates back to 1771. On August 27, 1877, a number of the Jonesport members of the Centre Street Congregational Church believed that the time had come for them to organize into a separate church and petitioned for acceptance of their request. Their request was voted upon, accepted and forwarded to Jonesport by Warren Hill, clerk of the Centre Street Congregational Church, on August 30, 1877.

On Tuesday evening, June 7, 1887, the Sawyer Memorial Congregational Church was dedicated "to the Everlasting God, our father." The Reverend E.L. Walbridge, first pastor of the new church, gave the invocation, and Mrs. George H. Mansfield provided the organ prelude for the service. The Reverend Daniel Green of Machias performed the scripture reading and prayer at the dedication.

The Honorable Daniel James Sawyer, a native of Jonesport, had decided with his wife several years before that a house of worship was needed, and a voice of God seemed to say to him, "Build unto me a House in which my children can worship." He proceeded to build and pay for all of the furnishings and was delighted to be able to provide this completed house of worship to his friends and neighbors in Jonesport, as well as to welcome visiting strangers to the new church. His generosity to the church continued until his death in 1909. In 1925, the church was named in his honor.

Sometime after 1910, nationally known philanthropist Andrew Carnegie offered to pay for half of the $3,000 pipe organ if the congregation would raise the other half. As a result of that gift and a number of ten- and fifteen-cent church socials and one-act plays, the needed funds were slowly raised to bring music to church services.

The first formal church wedding recorded was the marriage of Frances and Homer Worcester in 1927. The church has been well maintained through the years, and its white steeple can be clearly seen by the boats plying the waters of Chandler Bay. At night, its exquisite stained glass windows are illuminated to showcase the historic church's role in this Way Down East community.

All across America, hundreds and perhaps thousands who had the Country Churches Calendar for 2002 hanging in their home or office were privileged to see the Sawyer Memorial Congregational Church gracing the month of July. The photo used was from a postcard circa 1907.

The historic Sawyer Memorial Congregational Church serves the spiritual community of Jonesport–Beals Island.

The Sawyer Memorial Congregational Church continues to serve the spiritual needs of both year-round and summer residents of Jonesport and through its outreach program, the local Jonesport Food Pantry. The church is located at 28 Sawyer Square. For additional information, contact the pastor at jonesportsmcc@aol.com.

## JONESBORO

### *Jonesboro Union Church*

The area we know today as Jonesboro has a long history that even predates the native tribes having encampments along the shore of the Chandler River, which runs through the middle of present-day Jonesboro. The Vikings were the first to explore the area, and in the early 1600s, both the French and English were present.

The first settler to the area that had been designated by the Massachusetts General Court as Plantation 22 was Judah Chandler, who moved up from Scarborough in southern York County. He saw great potential for timber harvesting and built his home there in 1764. Plantation 22 includes what is today Jonesboro, Jonesport, Beals, Centerville, Roque Bluffs, the Kennebec section of Machias and Bucks Harbor in Machiasport. As new settlers arrived to the area along the Chandler River, the fledging settlement became known as Chandler River. Hannah and Rebecca Weston were two of the early settlers who earned historic recognition for their bravery in carrying lead and pewter for ammunition for the local Patriots to use to capture the British schooner *Margaretta* in the first naval battle of the Revolutionary War.

This small rural town in Washington County was named after John Coffin Jones, who had lost a sloop that had been part of America's disastrous naval defeat of the Revolutionary War at Castine. He was repaid for his loss by a land grant from the Massachusetts General Court of 48,160 acres, stretching from what is now Bucks Harbor to Jonesboro, including Roque Bluffs. The settlement was officially named Jonesboro in January 1789, and, on March 4, 1809, was incorporated as the town of Jonesborough by the commonwealth of Massachusetts. In March 1820, it became a town in the newly created state of Maine.

Historical records document that the Reverend James Lyon was the first minister to preach in the area, and the first sermon was given at the home of Captain Ephraim Whitney sometime before 1790.

Up until 1840, there was no church within the town of Jonesboro, but that year saw three churches organized within the community. On Thursday, April 24, 1840, in the home of Captain Joseph Sweetser, a Congregational Church was formed. May 1840 saw the organization of a Baptist Church, and on July 11, at 5:00 p.m. at the home of H.C. Hall, the First Universalist Society of Jonesboro was gathered. The spirit of ecumenical cooperation between different denominations did not exit in that era, and only the Congregational Church was able to fully form as the one church in Jonesboro.

The newly formed Congregational Church built its first meetinghouse in 1841 on property donated by John Tupper. A deed for the property was registered in the Machias Registry of Deeds in 1844. The building was configured as a twenty-six- by thirty-five-foot rectangular sanctuary with a steeple and bell tower. Entrance to the meetinghouse was on the west side of the building with the lectern at the rear. It accommodated twenty-four pews that were arranged in two rows with a center aisle. Each pew was assigned to a specific congregation family with an annual tax. Church records document that in 1893 each pew was assessed by Alden Varney at the rate of $1.46 to $2.92, dependent on its location. The following year, Joseph Drisko determined that the assessment needed to be raised to $1.89 to $3.78 to support needed repairs.

By the early 1900s, it had become obvious that the old meetinghouse needed a major renovation. This led to the organization of the Jonesboro Union Church Aid Society on March 12, 1909, with the goal of either building or repairing a house of worship, keeping it in good repair and providing for regular religious worship to be conducted in the building. Plans were immediately initiated by the newly formed Church Aid Society by hiring Portland architect Edward Leander Higgins to develop plans to renovate the old meetinghouse. To further the society's ambitious goals, they obtained additional land to their original plot in 1910 from the Lawrence Lumber Company, which allowed for the church to be set back on a stone foundation. By 1911, significant renovations had been completed, which included raising the building three feet, setting back twenty feet on a stone foundation and adding a vestry and vestibule, together with major changes in the church's seating arrangements. On July 7, 1911, with the major renovation project completed, the Jonesboro Union Church was formally dedicated.

During the 1920s, normal repairs to the church were made. The church was heated by a wood furnace and kerosene bracket lamps, and chandeliers provided lighting until electricity was installed in 1930. In spite of the hard times of the Great Depression, repairs and a new furnace were installed in the basement in 1938. Church attendance was very high during this period, as parishioners sought spiritual help in dealing with their economic plight.

From 1909 to 1961, the Church Aid Society was the governing body of the church, but in 1961, a new constitution was enacted, and the church officially became the Jonesboro Union Church. For the next two decades, the church joined with the East Machias Baptist Church to share a minister.

The week of July 9–16, 1995, was observed to celebrate the Jonesboro Union Church's 155th anniversary. At the dawn of the new millennium,

Jonesboro Union Church, Jonesboro: In 1909, the newly organized Church Aid Society hired Edward Leander Higgins, a Portland architect, to plan the remodeling of the old Union meetinghouse. By 1911, the church facility was completed.

the Jonesboro Union Church continues to provide a source of faith as well as family and individual counseling and other outreach programs. The Jonesboro Union Church is located at 24 Looks Point Road. For additional information, call (207) 434-2112 or e-mail pastorpam@gonowmail.com.

## Roque Bluffs

### *Roque Bluffs Community Chapel*

In 1776, a Scotsman named Schoppe, who had been a member of Burgoyne's army, defected to join the American cause for independence. He is believed to be the first settler in what we know today as Roque Bluffs. In the time prior to the Revolutionary War, a large area of present-day Washington County—that included Jonesboro, Jonesport, Beals, Centerville, Roque Bluffs, the Kennebec section of Machias and Bucks Harbor—was designated by the Massachusetts General Court as Plantation 22. This land grant included an area from Bucks Harbor to Jonesboro. Roque Bluffs was a part of Jonesboro from 1789 until 1891 when the people of the community voted to become a separate town. Mr. H.P. Gardiner from Boston, who owned Gardener's Island, asked that the newly formed town be named Roque Bluffs; historically the area had been known as Englishman's River.

During the early 1800s, settlers in the area and on the adjacent islands gathered together at various sites to worship. According to various documents, including diaries, logs and related journals that were handed down in families, this group was identified as the "Lamplighter Church."

In May 1840, Edmund Nugent, a Canadian minister, helped a small group in Jonesboro organize the Jonesboro Baptist Church. Since the newly formed church had no church building, it is believed that they held their worship services in a schoolhouse. During the period that Reverend Nugent served the fledging congregation, it grew from twenty-five parishioners to sixty-eight.

After Reverend Nugent departed from Jonesboro in the mid-1840s, not much is known about the church's activities. A document dated September

15, 1877, states that members of the English River group of the church voted for autonomy and to act separately, except when the action of the whole church deemed it necessary—for example, the election of officers and whether the assistant clerk should be located in Jonesboro.

Two years after the incorporation of the town of Roque Bluffs, the members of English River church group renamed themselves the Roque Bluffs Baptist Church. Mr. James Tupper donated land for the building of a church, and on June 24, 1904, construction of the church was initiated by Nathan B. Foster. The completed house of worship was dedicated on July 23, 1902. The Reverend Edward Long officiated at the dedication ceremony and became the church's first pastor. The pulpit for the new church was donated by Nathan B. Foster and the dais chairs by Mrs.E. Longfellow. The church's Ladies Aid Group was credited with collecting donations from summer residents in the amount of $500, which paid off the final construction debt.

The Roque Bluffs Baptist Church was deeded to the Washington County Baptist Convention to be held in trust on August 9, 1915. During the following years, services were held sporadically during the summer months when a visiting minister or theological student was in the area. To secure the church building during the years of the Great Depression, the building was deeded over to the United Baptist Convention of Maine, later known as the American Baptist Churches of Maine, on October 20, 1934. Later years saw the church building used for various community meetings and social activities, as well as Grange Hall for a brief period.

Worship services did not commence again at the church until the summer of 1985, when Eugene S. Watts started conducting services on a periodic basis during the summer months. He continued leading services at the church during the summer over the next five years.

Recently a group of dedicated women of Roque Bluffs, including Vicki Hooper, Ann Lockett, Eileen McKinnon, Hope Pratt and Marilyn Tenny, initiated a major renewal effort to save and restore the historic church building for the community. The group applied for and received a nonprofit corporate status from the state of Maine, and the American Baptist Churches of Maine deeded the property to the newly reregistered Roque Bluffs Community Chapel. The chapel is operated as an interdenominational ministry and is served by a volunteer clergy.

Most members of the community chapel maintain their primary church membership with their home church, while some consider the chapel their prime place of worship. Since its renewal, the chapel has been completely refurbished, including a new roof, a well and a septic system; handicapped accessible restrooms; and, for the first time, a heating system. The exterior of the chapel has been greatly enhanced by improved landscaping, including a meditation garden.

The chapel continues to grow in membership and in the number of worship services it provides, as well as in its outreach programs in the community. The chapel is also used for weddings, memorial services, gospel concerts and musical recitals.

The Roque Bluffs Community Chapel is operated today as an interdenominational ministry.

The Roque Bluffs Community Chapel is located at 3 Schoppee Point Road. For additional information, call (207) 255-6056 or send mail to Roque Bluffs Community Chapel, P.O. Box 471, Roque Bluffs, ME, 04654.

## MACHIAS

### *Centre Street Congregational Church*

The English first explored the area around Machias in 1633 and established a trading post there. The following year, the French who were vying to colonize the same area attacked the trading post, killed two of the six Englishmen and captured the others, taking away all of their merchandise. No attempt to colonize the area was undertaken by either the English or French for more than a century. Historical records show that the governor of Massachusetts visited the region in 1734, and in 1762, a group from Scarborough checked out the area for marsh grass, as a drought had devastated their hay crop. Here they found a great quantity, as well as an extraordinary amount of water power at the head of the tidewaters in addition to pristine forests for timber. On May 2, 1763, a small group from Scarborough landed on the shores of the Machias River to develop a permanent settlement. In 1767, the seventy-four settlers of Machias requested the Massachusetts General Court that their settlement be incorporated. Their request was granted in 1770.

The history of the Centre Street Congregational Church began in 1771 when the Reverend James Lyon began his ministry, as the first minister of the Gospel at Machias. He was the first settled minister east of the Penobscot River and a noted writer of musical compositions. He was not only a dynamic preacher and a strong leader but also a staunch Patriot for the American cause through the Revolutionary War era.

The first Protestant church in Machias was formed by six members, three men and three women on September 12, 1782. A barn standing opposite the site of the present church became the first meetinghouse. The sacrament of the Lord's Supper was first administered to these six initial communicants on October 6, 1772. The first church was built in

1774 on a lot at the end of Lyon Street where it enters Court Street. This church was known as the Little Brown Church on the Hill. A new church building was begun in 1794 and was completed in 1797. In 1836, a lot on Centre Street was purchased for $1,200 from George Smith for the site of the present church. Edward Shaw was chosen as the architect for the new neo-Gothic structure. The new church building was erected within one year for a cost of $12,500. The new meetinghouse was initially named the Centre Church but was later changed to the Centre Street Church. Captain Stephen Longfellow was chosen to obtain a bell for the new church. He traveled to Boston and found one of the famous bells cast by Paul Revere. This was not a new bell but one with a clear and mellow tone. This secondhand bell measures thirty-three inches from top to bottom and thirty-eight inches in diameter at its base.

In 1858, a separate vestry was built on Cooper Street and used for nearly three decades. When Centre Street was lowered in 1886, it resulted in the church basement becoming dry and habitable enough for a vestry. Musical interest was strong during the late 1850s. The church's first minister, the Reverend James Lyon, who was known as America's first hymnodist, and later William Bradbury, a noted composer and organist, were influential in shaping the church's musical heritage. The Organ Society was formed in 1859, and by the end of the Civil War, it had raised sufficient funds to purchase an organ. It contacted George Stevens, an organ builder from East Cambridge, Massachusetts, and purchased a tracker action organ at a cost of $2,300. It was shipped by boat to Machias in 1867. The new organ was installed in the rear of the church, and a dedication concert was held in May 1867 to celebrate its arrival. In 1889, the organ was moved to a new annex in the rear of the pulpit that accommodated both the organ and choir. The organ was hand pumped until 1933, when an electric blower was installed. This historic organ has remained in continuous use since that time.

The church was saved from destruction by fire in the fall of 1865 through the heroic efforts of the fire department. After the repairs were made, the church was rededicated in 1866. In 1870, a town clock with faces of seven feet in diameter was purchased and installed in the church's tower.

The memorial stained glass windows of the church arrived in Machias by train from the Colonial Glass Company of Boston in January 1899.

This Boston-based firm had adapted the art and technique developed by Tiffany to create the opalescent glass used in the memorial windows. A special service of dedication at the church was celebrated on August 6, 1899. There are eight large windows in the sanctuary and four smaller windows, two in the alcove and two on the streetside façade. The changes in light during the day have the effect of bringing life to the beautiful mosaics.

The Centre Street Congregational Church was listed on the National Registry of Historic Places in 1975, and on April 5, 1987, a special 150th anniversary service of celebration and rededication was held for the church edifice.

Recent years have seen major structural renovations made to the historic church. In 2001, the aluminum siding was removed and replaced by wooden clapboards that more accurately depict the church building's historical roots. The renovation project also included the restoration of the steeple, repair of the stained glass windows and a new roof. In 2006, a new addition was added to the church that houses an elevator that makes it accessible to all by bringing people up to the sanctuary. The architect designed the new addition to blend beautifully with the old building, as the angled windows on the front of the addition match the historic windows included in the church's design. The new addition was dedicated at a thanksgiving service during the Wild Blueberry Festival of 2006.

The Centre Street Congregational Church, Machias, was founded in 1772 and built in 1836.

The Centre Street Congregational Church has played both a major spiritual and community role in the Machias area for over two centuries. In addition to being the spiritual home of many local parishioners, the church's community activities include housing the Machias Area Food Pantry that is supported by the area churches, sponsoring various ecumenical worship services, hosting the annual Wild Blueberry Festival and sponsoring a variety of music concerts, as well as a number of other outreach programs.

The Centre Street Congregational Church is located on Centre Street. For additional information, contact the church by mail at Centre Street Congregational Church, United Church of Christ, P.O. Box 265, Machias, ME, 04654, by telephone at (207) 255-6665, by e-mail at centrechr@maineline.net or the website at www.centrestreetchurch.org.

### *Holy Name of Jesus Catholic Church*

Holy Name of Jesus Catholic Church in Machias has a rich historical tradition that is deeply weaved into the fabric of both the New England Catholic Church history and that of the state of Maine.

Just eight years after Maine was admitted to the Union and twenty years after Boston was established as a separate diocese, of which Maine became a part, Holy Name of Jesus Parish was formed in Machias in 1828. It preceded the establishment of the Catholic Diocese of Portland by twenty-six years. Prior to the building of the church in 1845, services were held in parishioners' homes by priests that covered the scattered Catholic missions of the diocese.

Bishop John Cheverus, Boston's first bishop, made yearly visits to Maine and ministered on these trips to both the small enclaves of Catholics and to the Penobscott and Passamaquoddy people. In 1804, Bishop Cheverus appointed Father Romagne as pastor to the two Indian nations and the scattered Catholic settlements in Maine. Father Romagne served in this role until 1824. In 1825, when Bishop Fenwick was consecrated as Boston's second bishop, he found only two priests in his diocese, a Father Byrne in Boston and a Father Ryan at St. Patrick's in Newcastle, Maine. In 1826, a Dominican priest, Father French, was stationed in Eastport. It is most likely that during Holy Name of Jesus's fledging years as a parish that Fathers Ryan and Ffrench were the priests that provided for the sacramental needs of the community.

Holy Name's historical roots here in Washington County can be traced back over four hundred years to the founding of the ill-fated French colony on De Monts Island on the St. Croix River near the present-day city of Calais. In July 1604, Mass was celebrated for the first time in New England by Father Nicholas Aubrey of Paris.

The present Holy Name of Jesus Church was built during the years 1875 and 1876 to replace the first church, which was destroyed by fire in 1875. The present church steeple was added at a later time.

As the Catholic population of southern Washington County grew, St. Michael's was built in Cherryfield in 1864 as a seasonal mission church to Holy Name of Jesus. Over the years, the Catholic population in the southern section of Washington County has continued to grow, and in 1990 the church building was moved to its new foundation and commenced operating year-round.

Holy Name Catholic Church, Machias, was built in 1875–76 to replace the first church that was destroyed by fire.

In 1936, the Cornelius Sullivan family of Whitneyville endowed the building of Our Lady of Mercies Church as a second mission church to Holy Name of Jesus. This church served the Catholic community of Whitneyville for thirty-six years until it was decommissioned by the Catholic Diocese of Portland in 1969. In 1996, the building was destroyed by fire.

At the dawn of this twenty-first century, the Catholic Church in America and here in Maine is seeing a low rate of priestly vocations, as well as an aging corps of priests to serve the spiritual needs of its parishioners. The outcome is that parish restructuring has begun and the era of the circuit riding priests has returned. The Reverend Eugene Gaffey, together with Deacon James Gillen, serves four churches of Cluster 10, Deanery III, here in Washington County within the recently structured St. Peter the Fisherman Parish. In addition to Holy Name of Jesus Church in Machias, this new parish entity includes St. Timothy's Church in Campobello Island, New Brunswick, Sacred Heart Church in Lubec and St. Michael's in Cherryfield. A distance of sixty miles separates St. Timothy's Church on Campobello Island from St. Michael's Church in Cherryfield. Holy Name of Jesus Church is located at 11 Free Street. For additional information, contact the parish office by mail at 11 Free Street, P.O. Box 248, Machias, ME, 04654-0248, by telephone at (207) 255-3731 or via e-mail at stpeterthefisherman@portlanddiocese.org.

## Machiasport

### *Bucks Harbor Baptist Church*

The town of Machiasport was settled in 1763 but was not officially incorporated as a town by the Maine legislature until 1826. The town served during its early history as the major port for the area. The community consists of three small villages of Larrabee, Bucks Harbor and Starboard. Among the incorporation warrants at the first town meeting was one with a specific reference to raise funds for the support of the Gospel ministry. This led the citizens of the community to build a meetinghouse in 1828.

The Reverend M. Dunbar in a letter to the local newspaper stated that the Machiasport Baptist Church, including Bucks Harbor, was organized in 1856 and that there were over forty members of the congregation at that time. He added that he had served as a part-time minister to the church since early in 1866.

During the late 1880s, there was a significant religious interest in the area. The Reverend Mr. Walbridge and the Reverend Mr. Harthorn, missionaries of the Baptist Convention, were holding revival meetings on a regular basis in both Bucks harbor and at Larrabee's Cove during the winter of 1886. On July 19, 1887, the Matthew brothers, who were known as the boy preachers, conducted services in Bucks Harbor. During the fall of 1887, George W. Lane of the Coast Missionary arrived in his yacht to address the Way-Side Sabbath School that he had organized six years earlier. On November 8, 1887, the Reverend J.D. Wilson of the Gospel Crusade preached at Bucks Harbor. In the spring of 1888, the newly formed Clerical Society in Bucks Harbor rented Vanity Hall for the purpose of holding religious services and meetings, and in late May 1888, F.S. Ames & Company supplied the society with seventy-two chairs. The Reverend D.B. Gunn held services in both Bucks Harbor and Larrabee's Cove during August 1888.

In November 1888, the Reverend Jesse B. Brown started preaching in both Bucks Harbor and Larrabee's Cove. The Bucks Harbor schoolhouse was the site for Reverend Brown's services from 1889 to 1891. It was in March 1891 that the congregation, together with Reverend Brown, had agreed on building a church in Bucks Harbor. Fundraising plans had been developed, and the ladies had formed a circle, pledging to help by holding suppers in the hall over F.S. Ames & Company's store or in the schoolhouse. Tickets for these benefit suppers cost twenty-five cents.

By November 1, 1892, about $400 had been pledged, and work on the foundation for the new Bucks Harbor Church had begun. Over two hundred feet of ditches for the foundation had been made and filled with rocks, while nearly three thousand bricks had been hauled in for use in the foundation by early December.

On January 17, 1893, Christian endeavor membership in the community was reported as follows: Bucks Harbor, thirty-nine; Larrabee, sixty-six; and Point of Maine, twenty-four. By February 13, 1894, records indicate that local membership had risen in Bucks Harbor to forty-five and in Larrabee to ninety-one, while Point of Maine's had dropped to thirteen. Work on the church continued, as did the task of raising funds for the project. By the late spring and early summer of 1894, the building was essentially raised. Enoch and Reuben Colbeth Jr. had done a considerable amount of work on this project, and Colbeth Jr. was credited with laying the cornerstone for the church. Work progress on the church edifice was reported as progressing well in March 1895. Mr.

A. Prescott had been working diligently on the project, and the southern end of the building had been finished and painted with two coats. One half of the clapboards were on the backside, the frame of the belfry was completed, the windows framed and the chimney installed and working. It took another year to complete the project.

On March 18, 1896, the Bucks Harbor Baptist Church was officially dedicated with a large attendance there to celebrate the new house of worship. The choir from the Port Village, with the assistance of organist Bertha Sanborn, provided music for the festive occasion.

For a century, the Bucks Harbor Baptist Church that the Reverend Jesse B. Brown helped build served the spiritual needs of many in the area. In the late twentieth century, it was decided that a new larger church was needed to meet the congregations need. Under the leadership of the Reverend Timothy Kinney Sr., a new modern church was built. In August 1999, the new church was dedicated. The Bucks Harbor Baptist Church continues to provide for the spiritual needs of its congregation and offers family movies and vacation Bible school to the community. The Bucks Harbor Baptist Church is located at 33 Ridge Road. For additional information, contact the pastor by telephone at (207) 255-6708 or visit the website at www.bucksharborbaptist.com.

The original Bucks Harbor Baptist Church, Machiasport, was dedicated on March 10, 1896.

## *Larrabee Baptist Church*

A little over ninety years from the first settlement of present-day Machiasport in 1763 and twenty-nine years after the town's incorporation, Baptists who lived in Bucks Harbor, Larrabee Cove and Starboard attended services at the First Baptist Church of Machiasport on the east side of the river. During the late 1880s, there was significant religious interest in the Bucks Harbor and Larrabee Cove areas, and a number of revival meetings were held. This led to the organization of the West Machiasport Baptist Church, which included Bucks Harbor, Larrabee and Starboard. The church building was built in Bucks Harbor to provide a central west-side location for worship.

On June 4, 1892, at the Bucks Harbor Church, the Reverend Day proposed the organization of an independent church at Larrabee Cove, which would be known as Larrabee Baptist Church. After much discussion, the proposal was postponed until July 2. It was postponed again until July 9, 1892, when permission was granted and letters of dismissal were given to sixteen members to move forward to organize the Larrabee Baptist Church.

The vision of having a Baptist Church in Larrabee Cove had existed in the minds and hearts of folks of the area for many years prior to the organizing of the church; this can be attested to by the fact that Charles Pettegrow had set aside a parcel of land at Larrabee Cove for a church in the early 1870s.

The Reverend H.F. Day served as Larrabee Baptist Church's first pastor. Church records show that, in 1893, a bell was installed in the church's belfry. This bell was replaced in 1910, but it too fell into disrepair; in 1989, considerable work was done to the belfry, which enabled it to be rung once again.

The historic Larrabee Baptist Church has served worshipping parishioners for well over a century, in both good and hard times. The church was struck by lightning on May 26, 1907, but thankfully was saved from tremendous damage. In 1911, a parsonage was built that served as the home of pastors for many years until it was sold to a local family. The church building has been kept in good repair with major renovation projects in 1912, 1983, 1989 and during the current era.

Larrabee Baptist Church, Machiasport, was established in 1892.

The Larrabee Baptist Church continues to shine as a beacon in the community. Its many outreach programs include its annual vacation Bible school. The Larrabee Baptist Church is located on Port Road (Route 92). For additional information, contact the pastor by telephone at (207) 255-6363 or visit the website at www.larrabeebaptist.org.

### *First Congregational Church of Machiasport*

The area we know today as Machiasport was, during the period before the Revolutionary War, part of a large area of present-day Washington County that was designated as Plantation 22 by the Massachusetts General Court. In 1826, the growing community of Machiasport separated from Machias and was incorporated as a town.

According to the records of Seth W. Lincoln, Esq., two years after Machiasport's incorporation as a town, some of the local residents who were down at Marston's Store one evening decided to build a meetinghouse. Custom of the time dictated that a town should have a meetinghouse. The next day they went out in the woods and cut the frame, and they continued to work on the project until the outside of the meetinghouse was completed. The interior of the building was finished during 1829. No records of the dimensions of the meetinghouse or the costs involved exist. It is believed, based upon oral history, that the outer appearance of the finished meetinghouse is essentially the same today as when it was built, replete with a belfry but lacking the steeple. The present front doors, east and west, opened into the vestibule that was divided by a large woodpile. A stairway led from the vestibule to a balcony, which was then used as a choir loft, while two inner doors led to the sanctuary.

A semicircular pulpit was elevated between three and four feet and was approached from the stairway. Behind the lectern were three seats for the minister and other dignitaries. To the right of the pulpit sat the tithing "tidy" man, with a long pole to gently tap any attendant found nodding off or any unruly youngster. The aisle placement has remained unchanged with all of the pews facing the pulpit. The wood stove that heated the meetinghouse was located in the rear of the building, and two beautiful windows captured the awesome view of the bay.

The official formation of the First Congregational Church of Machiasport dates to January 25, 1831, when William Palmer requested the formation of the church at meeting in the home of Jonathan Marston. A council was formed, with Josia Harris and Dennis Garland of the East Machias church present as delegates. A confession of faith was made at that time by Henry Cates, Mariah Cates, Daniel Palmer, Mary C. Palmer, Oliver Palmer, Samuel Small and John Sanborn Jr. On February 6, 1831, a letter came from the church in Machias, releasing a list of members and increasing the fledging church's membership to twenty-five.

The Reverend Gilman Bachella, a licensed preacher from Kennebec County, had been preaching in the area before the church had been organized, and he became the new church's first minister and clerk from January 12, 1831, until July 12, 1850.

Over the years, church records chiefly identify new members, baptisms, marriages, funerals and the election of delegates to represent the church at county and state meetings. The church records also show that some who were delinquent from attending church services were called in to give their reason for being absent, and a few were shown to have been excommunicated.

In 1963, the church received an inheritance from the estate of Nina Robinson Meech, which provided the funds to excavate under the church and build a room to use for church suppers and social gatherings. On December 2, 1966, Fellowship Hall was officially dedicated. The room has served a number of social gathering since then, as well as a place to hold services during the winter months.

The First Congregational Church of Machiasport for nearly two centuries has been the spiritual home to many residents of Machiasport. This beautiful historic church, sitting atop a steep bluff, possesses a commanding view of Machias Bay and has one of the most picturesque settings of any church in New England.

The First Congregational Church of Machiasport is located on Port Road (Route 92). For additional information, contact the pastor by telephone at (207) 255-3850.

The First Congregational Church of Machiasport, sitting atop steep hill with a commanding view of Machias Bay, has served as a meetinghouse for the port community since 1822.

## East Machias

### *Jacksonville United Methodist Church*

Methodism in Maine, and its relationship with the Jacksonville church, dates back to August 1, 1793, in Lynn, Massachusetts, when the New England Conference of Methodism held its easterly session there and established the province of Maine as a circuit. The Reverend Jesse Lee, an itinerant evangelist preacher, was appointed to the newly chartered circuit. He preached the first-ever Methodist sermon in Maine on September 10, 1793, at Sacco and went on to found a Readfield circuit on his first trip to Maine. On Reverend Lee's fourth circuit trip to Maine, he preached at Machias on April 27, 1795, and then journeyed onto the St. Croix Circuit. On his return trip to Massachusetts, he dedicated in Readfield the first Methodist Church in Maine.

The Reverend Lee was followed by other Methodist circuit riders. One of the best known of these courageous preachers was the Reverend Ebenezer Newell, who served on the St. Croix Circuit starting in 1819. In 1830, Reverend J. Hall was reported to have preached a sermon in East Machias, and two years later, the Reverend Moses P. Hill conducted services in both East Machias and Whiting. The Reverend H. Nickerson, presiding elder of the St. Croix Circuit, visited East Machias in 1833 and baptized Theophilas and Cordelia Doe. Their names were among the first to be members of the Jacksonville United Methodist Church. Early church records show that a Methodist Society was formed in East Machias in 1835 by the Reverend Moses P. Webster.

In 1836, the beginnings of the church came to fruition when the Reverend H.M. Macomber formed a class at both Upper Mills (Jacksonville) and at Lower Mills (East Machias). The following year, the two classes became a station served by the Reverend Charles Cone. During the early years of the fledging church, weekly class meetings were held in addition to the services conducted by the circuit rider preachers.

Through the 1840s and 1850s, services were held in the schoolhouse. During the pastorate of Reverend Nelson Whitney, a chapel was built on the present church site on land donated by Israel Hathaway in a deed dated November 1, 1858. Building of the chapel started in late 1858 and was completed and dedicated in 1859 by the Reverend Dr. Micah Jones Talbot, Providence, Rhode Island Conference.

In 1860, a parsonage and stable were built. The Reverend Caleb Ellis was very active with this building project, and it is believed that he was the first pastor to occupy it. A major remodeling of the church was undertaken in the late 1890s that included an addition with a memorial window and a belfry with a bell that rang out for the first time on October 15, 1897. Through the years, the church was kept in good repair, with electricity installed when electric power arrived in the area.

On September 10, 1958, the Jacksonville United Methodist Church community celebrated its centennial observance of the building of its chapel. Bishop John Wesley Lord of Boston and Superintendent Elwin Wilson of the Bangor District presided at this historic occasion.

Jacksonville United Methodist Church, East Machias, continues to grow to meet the spiritual needs of its parishioners.

Sunday, April 26, 2009, commemorated another historic moment in the spiritual life of the Jacksonville United Methodist Church, as it celebrated 150 years as a house of worship for the East Machias community. Bishop Peter Weaver of the New England Conference delivered a special message for this memorable event.

The Jacksonville United Methodist Church continues to carry out its mission at the dawn of the new millennium by teaching, preaching and sharing the good news of Jesus Christ and believing in the power of prayer to help transform lives, the church, the community and the world.

The Jacksonville United Methodist Church is located on Jacksonville Road. For more information, call (207) 255-6282 or visit the website at www.jacksonvilleumchurch.com.

## *First Congregational Church of East Machias*

In 1771, a few years before the Revolutionary War, the Reverend Lyons was called to minister to the people of West Falls (Machias), East Falls (East Machias) and Middle River (Marshfield). He served the three divisions of the area until his death. During those early days, the East Falls congregation met to worship in private homes, stores, barns and makeshift meetinghouses.

It was recorded at a town meeting in East Falls in 1786 that Mr. Peter Talbot offered to provide a lot of land on what was called Gun House Hill to the meetinghouse proprietors. Robert Gardner and his son, with their oxen, hauled stone and timber to the proposed building site, but strong objections were raised as to this location, and a new site where the present church stands was agreed upon. Mr. Talbot then moved all the building material to the new site.

In 1816, five years after the dedication of the new meetinghouse, citizens started to initiate talks of breaking away from the Union church. After East Machias was incorporated as a separate town in 1826, seventy-nine members meeting at the church in Middle River signed an application for withdrawal and then drew up articles of confession of faith and covenant to form their own church. On June 11, 1826, the new church group met to receive the first sacrament of the Lord's Supper. The Reverend Wales Lewis was called to serve the new church and preached to his new congregation for the first time on June 18, 1826.

The Union meetinghouse continued to be used for services by the new church group until they built their present house of worship in 1836. In the spring of 1837, the Revered Thomas Stone, the new church's first pastor, chose a pew for his family, and then the remaining sixty-three pews were auctioned off to members of the congregation to raise funds to maintain the church. A heated debate among members of the building committee took place as to whether the new edifice should have a spire or doors on the pews. The spire that adorns the church to this day won out. On April 5, 1837, the new First Congregational Church of East Machias was officially dedicated.

Through the years, the church building has been painted and renovated, including major repair work to the steeple that was almost

The First Congregational Church of East Machias was dedicated on April 5, 1837.

completely demolished by lightning in 1924. A capital campaign in 1948 allowed for the purchase of a new heating system, new carpeting and exterior painting.

The church's magnificent pipe organ that was purchased in 1872 is still played at services today. Listed in the National Register of Historic Buildings, its clock is one of the oldest tower clocks in Maine. In 1986, the Maine Historic Preservation Committee awarded a matching grant of $25,000 to refurbish the steeple. The Reverend Robert Blake, who was the church's pastor in the late 1970s and a watchmaker by trade, was able to reconstruct parts for the historic clock and get the hands to once again move.

Since its founding, the First Congregational Church of East Machias has played both a major spiritual and civic role in the community. It is located on High Street. For additional information, contact the pastor by telephone at (207) 255-3728.

## CUTLER

### *Cutler United Methodist Church*

Cutler, Maine, is a small rural fishing community on the Quoddy Loop. The Norse pool provides evidence that the Norsemen discovered this area long before Columbus sailed to the New World.

Overlooking the picturesque Cutler Harbor is the historic Cutler United Methodist Church. Since its founding in 1839 in this small fishing town, it has been a beacon of Christ's love to the community and an anchor of caring and hope to all.

The Reverends Mark Tuoll and James Thurston jointly conducted the first Methodist service in Cutler at the request of Mr. Freeman Maker. Under the leadership of Mr. John Olmore, the official church was formed in 1839. From its founding, the Cutler United Methodist Church conducted its worship services at the Head of the River Baptist Church until 1871.

The Reverend Joseph King became the fledging church's first appointed pastor in 1856 and was instrumental in the church's development.

In 1869, construction was started on the building that was to become the Cutler United Methodist Church. Unfortunately, the Saxy Gale of October 5, 1869, completely destroyed the structure. The following year, construction began again at a different location at the top of Meetinghouse Hill.

The church on Meetinghouse Hill served the Methodist congregation until 1911, when it was dismantled and rebuilt at its present, highly visible location. In 1913, the new Cutler United Methodist Church was officially dedicated by its pastor, the Reverend W. A. Swoozoy.

Many descendants of Cutler's first settlers, as well as descendants of the lighthouse keepers of the United States Lighthouse Service, who manned Little River Lighthouse in bygone days, are Cutler United Methodist congregation members.

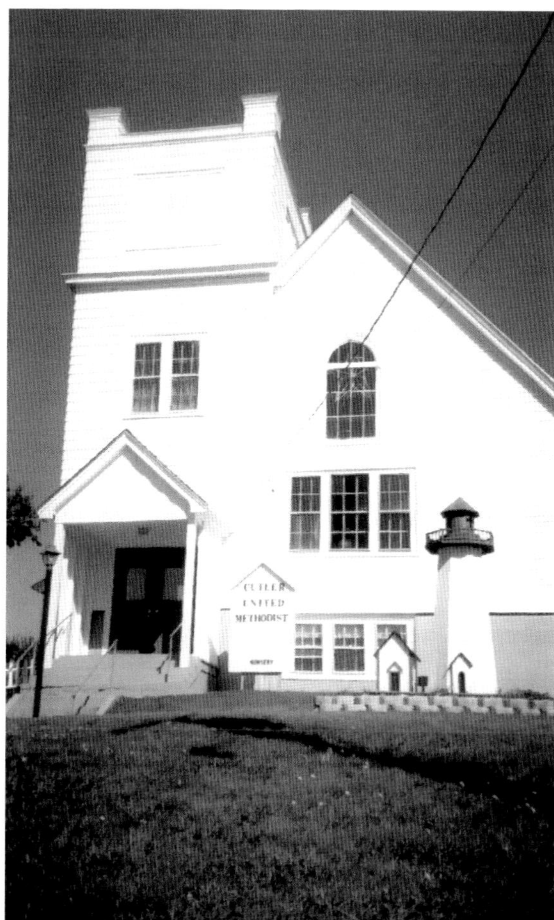

The current church was built in its present location, overlooking picturesque Cutler Harbor in 1913.

As a Christian beacon of faith and hope, the church continues to host community events and provide assistance. The church provides opportunities for fellowship for all with its many activities throughout the year.

The Cutler United Methodist Church is located at 2718 Cutler Road. For more information, call (207) 259-2097.

# LUBEC

## *Sacred Heart Church*

As early as 1811, a small number of Catholic families were scattered along the shores of Trescott. The Reverend Ephraim Abbot, a young missionary graduate from Andover Theological Seminary in Andover, Massachusetts, was assigned to do his mission work for the Society for Propagation of the Gospel to the early residents of this Way Down East region. He recorded in his diaries of 1811 and 1812 that he found in the area a number of Roman Catholics who were eager to hear the word of God from any source. A mission to the Passamaquoddy Indians at Pleasant Point had been established at an earlier time by the Jesuits. The Reverends John Lefeure Cheverus and Charles Ffrench were two of the early priests to serve in the Down East region. By 1825, many Irish immigrants were entering the United States through Eastport. Many of these new arrivals in America who settled in the Trescott area were from the Counties Antrim, Derry and Meath in Ireland.

By the early 1850s, a group of about fifty Catholic families were living in Trescott and were being served by priests from Machias and Eastport. A small chapel was erected at the site of the present Chapel Cemetery on Route 189 and Timber Cove Road. This chapel served as the spiritual home for this small Catholic community until 1881. Up until that time, fishing and farming were the main occupation for these people, but by 1881, the lead mines were in full operation; many families moved down from Trescott to West Lubec for employment in the new industry.

The population shift required a new church, and in November 1881, the Catholic women of Lubec and Trescott held a fair at Independence

Hall to raise funds for building a new church. It was reported in the Machias paper that the fair had netted $325 for their building project.

In 1882, a new mission church named St. Patrick's was completed at the head of Bay Road and Route 189. As the new century approached, Lubec's fishing industry was in full swing, and the Catholic population in Lubec was growing, which once again resulted in the need for a new house of worship closer into the town of Lubec. Thus the first Sacred Heart Church was built at the top of Main Street. The small new church served about twenty families. During this period, the Catholic community residing in Trescott, West Lubec and Lubec remained as a mission parish of Holy Name of Jesus Church in Machias.

In 1913, the mission parish status was transferred from Holy Name of Jesus Church in Machias to St. Joseph's Church in Eastport. At this same time, it was decided to form the Catholic congregations of Trescott, West Lubec and Lubec into a parish. The Reverend Joseph Sullivan began raising funds for this purpose. Bishop Joseph Walsh of the Diocese of Portland established Sacred Heart Church as a parish in 1914 and appointed the Reverend James A. Farley as its first resident pastor.

The Diocese of Portland, Maine, established Sacred Heart Catholic Church of Lubec in 1913.

By 1924, the first Sacred Heart Church had grown too small for its burgeoning population, and the parishioners began raising funds for a new and larger church. The Great Depression, with the market crash of 1929, put the building project on hold for nearly a decade. In the spring of 1937, ground was broken for the new Sacred Heart Church on the site of the old Fanning Homestead on Church Street. The new Sacred Heart Church was completed and free of debt in the fall of 1937. The first Mass was celebrated in the new church on November 7, 1937, and Bishop McCarthy dedicated the new Sacred Heart Church in June 1938.

Through the years, major projects were undertaken that included the building of a parish hall in 1967 and a new rectory in 1983. Today Sacred Heart Church in Lubec is a member of the newly structured St. Peter the Fisherman Parish and in Cluster 10, Deanery III, here in Washington County. For additional information, contact the parish office at Holy Name of Jesus Church by mail at 11 Free Street, P.O. Box 248, Machias, ME, 04654-0248, by telephone at (207) 255-3731 or via e-mail at stpeterthefisherman@portlanddiocese.org.

## *Lubec Congregational Christian Church*

Lubec is the easternmost town in the United States. It encompasses many miles of coastline, and at Lubec Narrows, Campobello Island, New Brunswick, is but a stone's throw away, though it was not until 1962 that a bridge connected Maine to this Canadian island. Lubec's first settlement was in 1780. The area became known as Flagg's Point and was so named according to legend for the first settler who had built a log cabin there.

The church's beginning dates to a few years after the settlement on Flagg's Point. In 1789, Lewis Frederick Delesdernier was appointed collector for the Federal Customs District of Passamaquoddy. Shortly after he set up his custom office at Flagg's Point, colonists from Moose Island (Eastport) started to settle on the islands of Passamaquoddy Bay and at North Lubec and Seward's Neck.

On July 29, 1811, the first town meeting of the town of Lubec, Massachusetts, was held at the home of Isaac Smith. Nine years later, Lubec became a town within the newly created state of Maine. During these early years, the Reverend Ephraim Abbott visited this Down East region doing mission work with the Society for Propagation of the Gospel and supplying Bibles and testaments to the settlers.

The War of 1812 resulted in the occupation of Eastport by the British in 1814. Many American Loyalists escaped from Eastport and resettled in Lubec. The period between 1815 and 1817 saw Lubec burgeoning into a thriving community, and with its development, a meetinghouse for the faithful was needed. During the summer of 1818, the Reverend Elijah Kellog of Portland came to Lubec as a missionary preacher and remained to serve for two and a half years. In September 1818, the church covenant was drawn up and signed, and subscriptions were taken up for the expense of building a meetinghouse. The following year, another pledge was established for the settling of a minister.

Lubec's first meetinghouse was the Congregational Church, which was completed on August 17, 1820. The architect for the new church was Mr. John Springer of Sterling, Massachusetts. The church was 55 feet in length, a breadth of 46 feet and a projection of 13 by 28 feet, with a spire of 125 feet. Unfortunately, the Saxby Gale of October 5, 1869, completely destroyed the spire. In 1872, a shorter spire was constructed.

On August 30, 1829, the Reverend Elijah Kellog preached the sermon at the dedication of Lubec's new meetinghouse that became fondly known as the "Big White." In April 1821, Mr. Jonathan Bigelow became the first settled minister.

From 1820 until 1856, the Big White was the spiritual home for the First Congregational Church and Parish Society. Around 1856, the meetinghouse was purchased by Jeremiah Fowler, and the First Christian Church moved into the building.

In 1931, at Seattle, Washington, the National Convention of Congregational Churches and the General Convention of the Christian Churches unanimously voted to unite the two bodies into the Congregational Christian Churches. The following year the First Christian Church in Lubec voted to change the local church to the Lubec Congregational Christian Church, encompassing fully the local heritage of the Big White meetinghouse.

The Big White meetinghouse, with its commanding presence, continues in this new millennium to be a spiritual home for many in the Lubec community. The Lubec Congregational Christian Church is located at

The historic Congregational Christian Church of Lubec was established in 1818.

46 Main Street. For additional information, contact the parsonage by telephone at (207) 733-2215.

## CAMPOBELLO ISLAND, NEW BRUNSWICK

### *St. Timothy's Catholic Church*

The earliest reference to religious life on Campobello Island can be traced the journal of Captain William Owen. He recorded that he had conducted an Anglican service in a shed for all the members of his new settlement on June 10, 1770. For the better part of the next century, the

Owen family ran Campobello Island as their own private fiefdom. The late 1880s saw the end of the Owen family saga and the beginning of the development of the island as a summer colony for wealthy families from Boston, Montreal, New York and Philadelphia. During the next decade, the Campobello Land Company constructed hotels and large private cottages for wealthy clients.

When the wealthy summer colony residents arrived at their cottages, they brought with them their household help. Many of these domestics were young Irish Catholics. A few of the summer colonists were also Catholic, as were some local residents. To meet the spiritual needs of this Catholic community, Mass was celebrated in private homes on an irregular basis.

In 1910, St. Timothy's Catholic Church was built in Welshpool by Monsignor O'Flaherty under the supervision of Bishop Casey. From 1910 until 1938, St. Timothy's was a mission church of St. Andrew's Parish, St Andrews, New Brunswick. In 1938, the mission assignment was transferred to Holy Rosary Church, St. Stephen, New Brunswick. A year later, St. Timothy's was made a mission of the St. John, New Brunswick, Cathedral Parish.

St. Timothy's church building also has a connection with the Owen family, as Grizel Cochrane, the daughter of Cornelia Ramsey Cochrane and granddaughter of Captain Robison Owen, was a major financial contributor for the building of the church in the memory of her mother.

Stained glass windows were obtained from St. Elizabeth's Church in Musquash, New Brunswick, which was being torn down and installed in 1936, along with a major renovation of the church's altar. Through the years, the church has been well maintained. Like most coastal communities, Campobello Island sees an influx of summer visitors; as an outcome, attendance at Mass increases dramatically at St. Timothy's during the summer months.

In 1977, an exchange was made between the Roman Catholic Dioceses of St. John, New Brunswick, and Portland, Maine, whereby the priest assigned as pastor to the neighboring Lubec, Maine church would administer to the spiritual needs of St. Timothy's parishioners. Through the late '70s and '80s, pastors at Sacred Heart Church in Lubec would joke that they were the only priests in the world who could say two midnight Masses on Christmas Eve. Many didn't understand that, although the two churches are only a short distance apart. Campobello Island, New Brunswick, is on Atlantic Time and Lubec on Eastern Standard Time, which accounts for an hour's difference, giving the priest ample time to get between the two churches to celebrate midnight Masses at each church.

Due to the low rate of priestly vocations, as well as an aging group of priests, the Roman Catholic Diocese of Portland found that they could no longer staff Sacred Heart Church in Lubec with a resident priest and needed to restructure the geographic area in order to meet the spiritual needs of Catholics in a broader area. This has resulted

St. Timothy's Catholic Church, Campobello Island, New Brunswick, was built in 1910 to provide for the spiritual needs of the island's Catholic community.

in the recent organizing of four churches of Cluster 10, Deanery III (Washington County) into a single parish. All four churches will continue to keep their respective names but collectively will be St. Peter the Fisherman Parish. St. Timothy's as a member of the new parish will have its spiritual needs provided by the Reverend Eugene Gaffey and Deacon James Gillen. For additional information, contact the parish office by mail at 11 Free Street, P.O. 248, Machias, ME, 04654-0248, by telephone (207) 255-3731 or by e-mail at stpeterthefisherma@portlanddiocese.org.

### *St. Anne's Anglican Church*

In 1787, David Owen, a nephew of the Captain William Owen, built a chapel on the highest point that was then called Whale Boat Cove, but later named Welshpool after the home village in Wales of the Owens.

Admiral William Fitzwilliam Owen, son of Captain Owen, was a lay reader who conducted Sunday services for the Anglican community for many years. Prior to the erection of St. Anne's Anglican Church in 1855, the admiral arranged for a priest to come to the island three or four times a year to administer the sacraments. Parish records contain entries in the admiral's handwriting of marriages he performed, as well as baptisms administered by priests during their annual visits.

On May 20, 1855, the Reverend John S. Williams officiated at the first public worship in the newly completed church. On September 18, 1855, the Right Reverend John Medley—first bishop of Fredericton, New Brunswick, a close friend of the admiral's and a frequent visitor to the island—consecrated St. Anne's church and church yard.

Since its establishment, over twenty-five clergy have served as rectors of St. Anne's.

In more recent memory, Campobello Island has become well known as a summer retreat for the Roosevelt family. It is here that the future president of the United States, Franklin Delano Roosevelt, spent his summers. As a young man, he would continue to return with his wife and family. Dore Schary's stage play *Sunrise at Campobello* and movie by the same name documented FDR's attachment to the island. Three generations of Roosevelts were summer parishioners of St. Anne's. A memorial plaque in memory of President Roosevelt is mounted on the west wall of the church.

FDR was not the only American president to worship at St. Anne's. In August 1966, President Lyndon B. Johnson and Mrs. Johnson, together with the Canadian prime minister Lester B. Pearson and Mrs. Pearson, attended service conducted by Archbishop Henry O'Neil of Fredericton, New Brunswick.

St. Anne's has a rich historical tradition. Among the many interesting points in the church is the font, which was created from a block of stone acquired from the Church of the Knights Templar at Malta. The stone was taken by Admiral William Fitzwilliam Owen's son-in-law, Captain J.J. Robinson, R.N., to Florence, Italy, where it was carved. The font dates from 1843. Many of the parish's communicants through the years have been buried in the churchyard, including Admiral William Fitzwilliam Owen.

St. Anne's Anglican Church, Campobello Island, New Brunswick, was consecrated by the Right Reverend John Medley in September 1855.

## Pembroke

### *St. John the Evangelist Catholic Church*

Pembroke lies on the northwest side of Lubec Bay in the eastern section of Washington County. It was first settled in 1774 by Hatevil Leighton, a native of Gouldsborough, Maine (Massachusetts at that time). Pembroke was a part of Dennysville until its separation and incorporation as a town on February 4, 1832.

In the year of the town's incorporation, General Ezekiel Foster, an entrepreneur from Eastport, initiated the building of the Pembroke Iron Works. The building to house the new enterprise was 171 feet wide and 160 feet long and was powered by falls that flowed into Cobscook Bay. The works were operated for a few years by Foster and Bartlett and then sold to Gray & Company of Boston. In 1849, the enterprise was sold to William E. Coffin & Company of Boston. The iron works produced about five thousand tons of iron yearly for products such as nails, horseshoes and boiler rivets.

Tucked away on Achill Island off the west coast of County Mayo, Ireland, was the labor force that was to come and man this new enterprise. Newly arrived Irish immigrants found Pembroke to be quite similar to their ancestral homeland and encouraged more friends and relatives to come and partake in the work opportunities that the iron works offered.

The Pembroke Iron Works helped spawn an economic boom to the area and became its major industry, starting around 1860. On February 14, 1883, the ironworks agent's house was destroyed by fire. This event set in motion the decline of the company. By 1887, Pembroke Iron Works was history.

By 1850, a Catholic community was well established in Pembroke, and in 1855, the present St. John the Evangelist Church was built as a mission church of St. Joseph's Eastport. The interior of St. John's remains essentially unchanged with its high back pews. The altar is one that was originally at St. Joseph's. Heat and electricity have been added. The church was still heated by a wood stove in the front of the church until the 1980s. In fact, the family that saw to it that the stove had been lit to heat the church for Mass continues the family tradition by turning on and off the present oil heating system.

The years from 1828 to 1860 are referred to as the circuit riding period for priests serving parishioners Way Down East, Maine. St. John the Evangelist Church in Pembroke and St. Michael's in Cherryfield are the only two remaining Catholic churches that architecturally reflect the mission period of the pre–Civil War era. Church records dating back to the circuit riding days indicate that churches existed back then in both Robbinston and Trescott. In fact, a Catholic cemetery was located in Trescott. Today St. John the Evangelist Church has the only Catholic cemetery in Washington County. A walk through this historic cemetery while taking time to view the old gravestones will provide one with a wealth of the Celtic heritage.

To commemorate St. John the Evangelist's Irish Catholic presence in Pembroke, a Celtic cross was placed on the church during the 1990s. Exterior painting work is currently underway to restore the church to its Victorian-era appearance.

St. John the Evangelist Catholic Church, Pembroke, was built as a mission church of St. Joseph's Eastport to serve the newly arrived Irish immigrants.

The gravestones of St. John the Evangelist Cemetery provide an insight into the close community the Irish immigrants made in their new land.

St. John the Evangelist will continue to keep its present name and be a mission to St. Joseph's in Eastport, but under the diocesan reorganization, it will be part of the new spiritual unit: the Parish of Blessed Kateri Tekakawitha, which includes the Catholic churches in Eastport, Pleasant Point, Calais, Baileyville and Indian Township.

For additional church information, contact St. Joseph's rectory in Eastport by telephone at (207) 853-2825 or via e-mail at stjosepheastport@verizon.net.

## Eastport

### *St. Joseph's Catholic Church*

Here in the easternmost city of the United States is St. Joseph's Catholic Church. It was established in 1818 and is the third oldest Catholic Church in Maine and one of the oldest Catholic Churches in New England. Being located in this eastern section of Washington County makes St. Joseph's historical roots date even further back to 1604, when Samuel de Champlain and his fellow French explorer Sieur de Monts founded the ill-fated St. Croix Island settlement about fourteen miles upriver from present-day Eastport. In July 1604, Father Nicholas Aubrey of Paris celebrated the first Mass in this region of the New World. Members of the Passamaquoddy tribe assisted these French settlers, and as a result of this contact and other early seventeenth-century missionary work, the Passamaquoddy people embraced Catholicism.

By 1789, Moose Island was home to twenty-two families. Eight years later, in 1797, the settlers of the area petitioned the legislature of the commonwealth of Massachusetts to be incorporated as the town of Freetown. The legislature ignored their town name request but incorporated the community as Eastport on February 24, 1798.

Eastport's close proximity to Pleasant Point, the land established by the treaty of 1794 as belonging to the Passamaquoddy Nation, has linked the religious life of two adjoining communities. Shortly after the American Revolution, John Carroll, the first Catholic bishop of America, answered the request of the Passamaquoddy people for a priest and sent Father John Lefevre de Cheverus, who was later to become the first bishop of New England to meet their spiritual needs with periodic visits. When Father Cheverus made his visits to Pleasant Point, he also tended to the spiritual needs of Irish families living in Eastport.

In 1826, ecclesiastical responsibility for churches in Maine was transferred from the bishop of Quebec to the diocese of Boston. Father Charles Ffrench, a fifty-one-year-old Irish Dominican priest arrived in Eastport and was given pastoral responsibility for the entire Maine coast, from Eastport to Dover, New Hampshire. He quickly moved to build churches in Eastport, Portland and Dover. The cornerstone of St. Joseph's was laid on April 29, 1828, and on June 13, 1828, St. Dominic's cornerstone was set in Portland.

The first Mass was celebrated in the unfinished fifty- by thirty-two-foot St. Joseph's Catholic Church in 1829. It was not until 1835 that St. Joseph's was dedicated. There were about three hundred Catholic parishioners at this time in Eastport. Unfortunately, most were quite poor, and the parish was on shaky financial ground from its beginnings and owed a local carpenter $1,100 for construction of the church and rectory.

During the last third of the eighteenth century, the Catholic population of Eastport grew, requiring the need for a new larger church. The original 1828 church building was moved across the street to become the parish hall, which it still functions as today. In 1874, the second St. Joseph's Church was completed. With the economy booming and the population continuing to expand, the church required additional space. In 1885, the present rectory was built, while during 1887–88, construction took place that raised the church by four feet and lengthened it by thirty feet.

A Hook and Hastings pipe organ was installed, and other improvements were made, including a heating system, electric lights and a new bell to replace an earlier bell in the steeple. A chapel and a music room were also added during this late eighteenth-century period.

In the period preceding the stock market crash of 1928 and the start of the Great Depression, St. Joseph's Church replaced the windows of the church with breathtaking stained glass windows that portray the life of Christ, while the windows in the steeple behind the organ are designed with a musical motif. During this same period, paintings depicting the Stations of the Cross were hung in 1925. They still remain in the church today.

The Great Depression hit Eastport and St. Joseph's hard and started a migration from the area. By 1937, the average Sunday collection had dropped to $24.36. Eastport's population continued to shrink and, by 1960, had lost 25 percent of its pre-1940 population.

During the 1970s, St. Joseph's underwent further renovations, including the restoration of the sanctuary to its nineteenth-century beauty while keeping it in harmony with Vatican II's liturgical requirements.

For nearly two centuries during both good and hard times, St. Joseph's has been a community of church for its parishioners and visitors, as well as an active ecumenical partner with sister churches in Eastport.

In this, the first decade of the twenty-first century, the Catholic Church in both America and Maine is faced with both a low rate of priestly vocations and an aging clergy. In 2006, Bishop Richard Malone of the Portland Roman Catholic Diocese unveiled a plan to reorganize Maine's 139 parishes into clusters. Here in eastern Washington County, churches in Eastport, Pleasant Point, Pembroke, Calais, Baileyville and

St. Joseph's Catholic Church, Eastport, was established in 1818 and is Maine's third oldest Catholic Church.

Indian Township have been grouped together as one spiritual unit. Each church will keep its respective name, but all of these churches within the spiritual unit are now one parish—the Blessed Kateri Tekakwitha parish. The Blessed Kateri Tekakwitha was a Mohawk woman who had been evangelized by Jesuit missionaries in New York. St. Joseph's will continue to serve the spiritual needs of its community within its new parish role. As a church within the Parish of Blessed Kateri Tekawitha, it is a part of Cluster 8 and Deanery III in Washington County.

For additional information, reach the parish rectory in Calais by telephone at (207) 454-0608.

## Robbinston

### *Grace Episcopal Chapel*

Robbinston, Maine, is a small rural community on the St. Croix River between Perry and Calais. It was first settled in 1786. It is close to St. Croix Island, the site of the ill-fated French settlement of 1604 that was led by Sieur de Mons and Samuel de Champlain.

During the last half of the nineteenth century, areas on the Quoddy Loop became summer retreats for many wealthy Americans and Canadians. Robbinston on the St. Croix River became a popular summer colony during this period.

To fulfill the spiritual needs of these summer visitors, the Reverend Dr. Peter H. Steenstra of Cambridge, Massachusetts, founded Grace Episcopal Chapel as a summer chapel.

The former Grace Episcopal Chapel was built in 1882. Its Carpenter Gothic architecture makes it a historic gem, and on August 7, 2001, it

Grace Episcopal Chapel, Robbinston, was founded by the Reverend Dr. Peter H. Steenstra of Cambridge, Massachusetts, in 1882 to serve as summer chapel for both year-round and summer residents.

was added to the National Register of Historic Places. Today it serves as a cultural destination for Down East travelers.

Grace Episcopal Chapel is located on U.S. Route 1 one and a half miles northwest of its junction with Third Street.

## Calais

### *Immaculate Conception Church*

No further information of a Catholic presence in the Calais area is found until St. Joseph's Church in Eastport was established in 1826.Various missionaries visited Calais during the period from 1830 to 1859, when the parish was established. It is believed that the first Mass celebrated in Calais was at the home of John Tracy in 1830 by a Reverend McMahon. There was not a priest by the name of McMahon at St. Joseph's in Eastport, but at the time, Father Patrick McMahon was the pastor of a St. John, New Brunswick parish and most likely the priest mentioned in accounts from that period. Subsequent Masses were said to have been held at the residence of Mr. Dunn on Chandler Street and at the River View House.

In August 1852, the old town hall on Union Street was purchased from the recently incorporated City of Calais as a house of worship for the fledging Catholic population. The building was totally refitted to serve in its new role. Many details of this period that were part of the diocesan records were unfortunately lost in the Portland Fire of 1866. According to a survey completed for Bishop Healy in 1875 by the Reverend Conlon, the church was dedicated between 1852 and 1855 by the Reverend Basil Pacciarini, S.J., a missionary who visited Calais on numerous occasions during that period. The official date for the founding of the parish is 1859 when Father Murphy was assigned as resident pastor.

In 1864, Bishop Bacon dedicated the church after interior renovations had been made and a bell installed in the bell tower. Five years later, a property on High Street was purchased from Isaac W. Bradbury for a rectory. During the 1870s, there were thirty or forty Catholics living in the Robbinston and Red Beach area. To meet the spiritual needs of these Catholics, the Chapel of the Holy Cross was erected in Robbinston between 1873 and 1880 by the Reverend Patrick Reardon, who was the assistant to Father Conlon.

The convent school was erected in 1884 at a cost of $14,000. The Sisters of Mercy arrived to staff the school on August 5, 1885, and Bishop Healey dedicated the school in September when it opened for students. The school remained in operation until 1969, and having badly deteriorated over the years, it was demolished in 1983 to make way for a new church.

Immaculate Conception Parish had its first church specifically built as its house of worship on Calais Avenue in 1893 at a cost of $18,000. The first Mass was celebrated on Christmas Day 1893 by Father Michael F. Walsh. On September 30, 1894, Bishop Healey dedicated the new church. Two years later a rectory was built next to the church.

For nearly a century, the Calais Avenue church served the parishioners of Immaculate Conception. In April 1987, a fundraising campaign was initiated to build a new church. On Easter Sunday 1987, groundbreaking on the site of former convent school took place for the new edifice. Dearborn and Whited of Portland were selected to design the new church, and Oulette Construction Company of Madawaska was awarded the building contract for $930,641. The new, more energy efficient, multifunctional, 4,500-square-foot facility included the new church, church hall, classrooms and rectory. On August 7, 1988, Bishop Edward O'Leary dedicated the new church. During the 1990s, a bell tower and a prayer garden were added.

On the evening of July 23, 2005, lightning struck Immaculate Conception Church. Many parishioners stood by the side of the road, watching flames engulf their church and burn it to the ground. Nearly everything in the church and rectory was destroyed except for the statue of the Virgin Mary, which survived with only minor damage. The neighboring First Congregational Church of Christ graciously opened their doors to its displaced Catholic neighbors and provided a home for Catholics to hold Mass until Immaculate Conception could be rebuilt. Three years later, Bishop Richard Malone of the Portland Diocese dedicated the new church. Joining the bishop for the dedication were fifteen priests from across the diocese, area Protestant

The old town hall on Union Street, Calais, was purchased from the city and refitted as the first Immaculate Conception Catholic Church in August 1852.

clergy and members of the Jewish faith, as well as more than four hundred parishioners.

All business for the Parish of the Blessed Kateri Tekawitha will be handled from the Immaculate Conception Church office in Calais at 31 Calais Avenue. The office mailing address is P.O. Box 898, Calais, ME, 04619-6908. For additional information, call (207) 454-0680 or e-mail bk2008@myfairpoin.net.

## *St. Anne's Episcopal Church*

In April 1604, Pierre Dugua, Sieur de Mons, sailed from Havre de Grace, France, aboard the flagship *Bonne Renomee*, bound for North America. King Henry IV granted Dugua a trading monopoly and the title lieutenant general of New France. In exchange, Dugua was directed to establish name, power and authority of the king of France; to summon the natives to the Christian religion; to cultivate and settle the lands; and to make explorations and especially to seek out mines of precious metals. In June, Pierre Dugua, Samuel Champlain and seventy-seven other men, including a Catholic priest and a Huguenot minister, arrived in the New World and established a settlement on St. Croix Island, just off from present-day Calais, Maine. The winter of 1604–05 was harsh and nearly half of the colonists perished. In the spring of 1605 the surviving colonists moved to Port Royal, Nova Scotia. As an outcome of this ill-fated settlement, Christianity did not return to the Calais area for a lengthy period of time.

The place we know today as the city of Calais was first settled in 1779 by a Daniel Hill, who moved up from Jonesboro to what was then called Township Number 5. In 1809, Calais was incorporated as a town, and in 1850, it was incorporated as a Maine city, with George Downes as its first mayor. This border city was burgeoning during the mid-nineteenth century.

St. Anne's congregation beginnings can be traced to a series of meetings in the mid-1850s that were held on the second floor of Horton Hall on Main Street in Calais. On November 24, 1850, these early meetings of the congregation were moved to the present location on Church Street, where the church hall still stands.

It soon became apparent that a permanent house of worship was needed, and on June 10, 1853, the cornerstone for the new church was laid. The church, a wood-frame structure of Gothic architectural style, was designed by the prominent architect of the time, James Renwick, who designed St. Patrick's Cathedral in New York City and the original Smithsonian Institute building in Washington, D.C. St. Anne's was consecrated on May 11, 1854, and has been in continuous service since then.

St. Anne's Church has a seating capacity of 150 and a tower with a four-face clock and working bell, as well as an electric organ. As the result of a major fundraising program and many hours of volunteer work, the parish has recently restored major portions of the church and clock tower. This Carpenter Gothic–style church was added to the National Registry of Historical Landmarks on July 8, 1982.

May 2007 saw the construction of a new parish hall to better meet the needs of today. The new parish hall is a multifunctional facility with a rector's study, Christian education/library office, church office, choir room, nursery with restroom, two handicap bathrooms, sacristy, double classroom, janitor's room, utility room and the Great Hall. The building's new heating system also services the church.

St. Anne's Episcopal Church in Calais was consecrated on May 11, 1854, and has provided continuous spiritual service since then.

St. Anne's rectory is a ten-room wood-frame colonial house located on a spacious lot on Lafayette Street four blocks from the church and is home to the resident priest. St. Anne's Episcopal Church is located at 23 Church Street. For additional information, contact the parish office by telephone at (207) 454-8016.

*Chapter 4*

# Passamaquoddy and Penobscot Spiritual Traditions

## Indian Township, Pleasant Point and Indian Island Reservations

For thousands of years, the indigenous people in what is now maritime Canada and Maine included the Passamaquoddys, Maliseet, Mi'kmaq, Abenaki and Penobscot tribes. These native people belonged to a loose confederation known as the Wabanaki Alliance, but all continued to maintain their respective sovereignty. Today most Passamaquoddy people live in two relatively small communities in Washington County. Indian Township, near Princeton, is divided into two sections: the section of the reservation that is located on present-day Route 1 is known as the strip, and the section bordering Grand Lake Stream is the Peter Dana Point settlement. The second community is Pleasant Point on Passamaquoddy Bay near Perry. Prior to the Treaty of 1794, the Passamaquoddy tribe's land extended from Point Lepreau in New Brunswick to Schoodic on the north and west, past the Machias River to Mount Desert. Passamaquoddy, or Peskotomuhkati, a major dialect of the Algonquian language, was the language spoken by the Passamaquoddy people. It is believed ancestors of current tribal members lived in present-day Down East Maine more than twelve thousand years ago. Ancient art depicting their history and culture is found in three-thousand-year-old petroglyphs carved in rocks

Blessing the ancient petroglyphs at the water's edge.

Honoring the return of the ancient petroglyphs site.

at a shorefront site off Clark Point (formerly Birch Point) in Machiasport. In October 2006, this historic and spiritual site was returned to the Passamaquoddy Nation.

The Penobscot Indian people today live on Indian Island near Old Town. The reservation is surrounded by the waters of the Penobscot River. This major Maine river runs from the Penobscot's sacred Mount Katahdin down to Penobscot Bay. The people's heritage and identity are directly tied to the river. Their treaty with Massachusetts in 1796 resulted in the loss of all their land in the Penobscot Valley. They were left with only two acres in Brewer, the islands in the Penobscot River above Old Town, two coastal islands and land near present-day Lincoln, Howland and Millinocket. The Penobscot people spoke an Eastern Abenaki dialect of the Algonquin language. Penobscot originates from a mispronunciation of their name Penawapskewi. Their name means descending ledges or rocky part and originally referred to a specific section of the Penobscot River between Bangor and Old Town. In the spiritual traditions of the Penobscot people, Mount Katahdin is so sacred that it would be totally

Celebrating the traditions.

sacrilegious for one of them to climb to the top of the mountain. They believe that the highest god in their spiritual system, Glukab sent the lower angry god, Pamola, to Pamola Peak for eternity because of his bad behavior. Penobscot art reflects the people's close relationship with nature. The fiddlehead is considered a delicacy, as well as one of the first plants to bloom in spring, and is the insignia for the Penobscots. The fiddlehead is considered by the Penobscots to be a gift from a higher power for having survived the winter.

In June 1604, a French Jesuit named Father Nicholas Aubrey, accompanied Pierre Dugua, Sieur de Mons and Samuel Champlain, a group of explorers, established the first European settlement north of St. Augustine, Florida, on Saint Croix Island just off present-day Calais, Maine. The French settlers who survived the horrible winter of 1604–05 were saved and helped to relocate to Port Royal, Nova Scotia, in the spring by the local Passamaquoddy. Father Aubrey was one of the many colonists who perished, but he was instrumental during the summer and fall of 1604 in converting the Passamaquoddy people. After Father Aubrey's death and the departure of the colony, the Passamaquoddy people continued to practice their new Christian faith without a priest for over sixty years. In the late 1600s, priests would make annual visits to celebrate Mass and perform baptisms and marriages.

In 1723, during the Dummers War, Father Sebastian Rasle, S.J., a missionary who lived in a Wabanaki village at Norridgewock and had been active in making the tribe's complaints known to the authorities, was scalped and mutilated by British soldiers to make it appear he was murdered by Indians. Oral history also details that an Indian named One-Armed Nikola took the iron cross from the local church and carried it off to Indian Island for safety.

When the French and Indian War ended in 1760, French Jesuits were no longer permitted to provide for the spiritual well-being of the Passamaquoddy and Penobscot people. Many Indian Catholics traveled to Quebec to have a priest marry them and baptize their children.

The Penobscots went to Baltimore and requested that the bishop send a priest to minister to them on Indian Island. The bishop sent a Jesuit missionary (a black robe) to serve the Wabanaki confederacy of tribes in what is now Maine and Canadian maritime provinces.

During the Revolutionary War, the Passamaquoddy and Penobscot tribes joined forces with the American Patriots in their fight for independence. After gaining their independence from England, the General Court of the commonwealth of Massachusetts provided a salary to Father James Romagne to minister to the Passamaquoddy and Penobscot people.

During the early 1800s, churches were built on Indian land. The mid-1800s represented the second phase of black robe missionary work in Maine. According to Father John Bapst, S.J., there were only four diocesan priests in the state, and everywhere above Portland was a mission in 1852. At that time, there were thirty-three towns or circuits, but only a few had churches, including the chapels at Pleasant Point, Peter Dana Point and Indian Island.

The churches at Pleasant Point, Peter Dana Point and Indian Island are each named for St. Ann, the mother of Mary and grandmother of Jesus. The churches' name shows the reverence that Indians have for their ancestors. In September 2008, the Passamaquoddys celebrated the 160th anniversary of St. Ann's Church at Peter Dana Point, Indian Township, by recreating the canoe trip that took their first priest, Father Vetromile, from the strip section of Indian Township to St. Ann's Church at Peter Dana Point. Directly across from the church is one of Washington County's oldest cemeteries, with markers dating prior to 1848.

St. Ann's at Peter Dana Point has a beautiful mural behind the altar that depicts the community as it was in bygone days. An eagle grasping a cross plays a dominant role in this mural, as the eagle is an important spiritual symbol in both Christianity and in native culture. In Christian tradition, the eagle represents the Gospel of St. John, and to Indians, the eagle serves in a similar role as angels as a messenger from God, as well as a symbol of the soul rising to heaven. In keeping with native tradition, dream catchers are hung from the church's chandelier.

St. Ann's Church at Pleasant Point has a stained glass window depicting Blessed Kateri Tekawitha, a Mohawk woman who had been evangelized by Jesuit missionaries in upstate New York. Another stained glass window depicts a black robe surrounded by North America martyrs.

The Penobscot's church on Indian Island has no crucifix behind the altar but a painting of a crucifixion scene that was painted by a

St. Ann's Church at Pleasant Point.

Penobscot more than two hundred years ago on two pieces of altar cloth that he stitched together for his canvas. He made his own paints from dyes derived from barks, plants and berries. In his painting, he portrayed Jesus's and Mary's facial features to resemble those of native people.

Nuns arrived during the late nineteenth century to provide both a secular and religious education for the children on the reservations. They continued their teaching at reservation schools for nearly one hundred years until a low rate of vocations resulted in their inability to staff the schools.

In July 2008, St Ann's Churches at Pleasant Point and Dana Point, Indian Township, were grouped together with churches in Eastport,

Spiritual dance in front of sweat lodge.

Pembroke, Calais and Baileyville as one spiritual unit. Each church within this reorganized cluster will continue to maintain its own name but the total new group is now collectively called Blessed Kateri Tekawitha Parish with one priest to serve this spiritual community. For additional church information, contact the parish rectory by mail at 31 Calais Avenue, P.O. Box 898, Calais, ME, 04619-6908 or by telephone at (207) 454-0680.

In 2009, St. Ann's Church on Indian Island was grouped with churches in Old Town, Orono and Bradley to form a new spiritual community known as the Parish of Resurrection of the Lord. All of the churches will continue to maintain their individual church names as part of the Portland Catholic Diocese Cluster 29 in Deanery IV for Southern Penobscot, Hancock and Waldo Counties. For additional information about St. Ann's Church, Indian Island, contact the parish office by mail at 429 Main Street, Old Town, ME, 04468 or by telephone at (207) 827-4000.

# About the Authors

Jim and Jane Diggins Harnedy have lived in their adopted state of Maine for over thirty years. Jim is a native of Brookline, Massachusetts, and a retired computer industry executive. Jane was born in New York City but moved to the Boston suburb of West Roxbury as an infant. Jim received his bachelor's degree in history from Boston College and did graduate work at both Georgetown University and Framingham State College. After working for a number of years in the administrative field of mental health, Jane decided to fulfill a lifelong dream of becoming an artist and started taking art instruction under several nationally known seascape artists. She later attended the University of Maine at Augusta and has operated her own gallery, the Blue Lobster, for over thirty years. Jim and Jane are the parents of two daughters and have four grandchildren and nine great-grandchildren. Through the years, they have worked on a number of creative projects together. They live Way Down East at the water's edge in Bucks Harbor, Machiasport.

## Other Books by Jim and Jane Diggins Harnedy

*Images of America: The Boothbay Harbor Region* by Jim Harnedy (Arcadia Publishing)

*Images of America: Around Wiscasset* by Jim Harnedy (Arcadia Publishing)

*Scenes of America: The Boothbay Harbor Region* by Jim Harnedy (Arcadia Publishing)

*A Handy Guide for Eucharistic Ministers* by: Jane Diggins Harnedy with Jim Harnedy (ALBA House)

*Images of America: The Machias Bay Region* by Jim and Jane Diggins Harnedy (Arcadia Publishing)

*Images of Canada: Campobello Island* by Jim and Jane Diggins Harnedy (Arcadia Publishing)

*Scenes of America: The Machias Bay Region* by Jim and Jane Diggins Harnedy (Arcadia Publishing)